William Shakespeare's ROMEO AND JULIET

Leonard Jenkin
Department of English
Columbia University

1997 Barnes & Noble Books

MACMILLAN is a registered trademark of Macmillan, Inc.
Monarch and colophons are trademarks of Simon & Schuster, Inc.,
registered in the U.S. Patent and Trademark Office.

Macmillan Publishing USA
A division of Simon & Schuster, Inc.
1633 Broadway
New York, NY 10019

ISBN 0-7607-0654-9

Text design by Tony Meisel

Printed and bound in the United States of America.

00 01 M 9 8 7

RRDC

CONTENTS

INTRODUCTION

FACTS VERSUS SPECULATION

Anyone who wishes to know where documented truth ends and where speculation begins in Shakespearean scholarship and criticism first needs to know the facts of Shakespeare's life. A medley of life records suggest, by their lack of inwardness, how little is known of Shakespeare's ideology, his beliefs and opinions.

William Shakespeare was baptized on April 26, 1564, as "Gulielmus filius Johannes Shakspere"; the evidence is the parish register of Holy Trinity Church, Stratford, England.

HUSBAND AND FATHER

On November 28, 1582, the Bishop of Worcester issued a license to William Shakespeare and "Anne Hathwey of Stratford" to solemnize a marriage upon one asking of the banns providing that there were no legal impediments. Three askings of the banns were (and are) usual in the Church of England.

On May 26, 1583, the records of the parish church in Stratford note the baptism of Susanna, daughter to William Shakespeare. The inference is clear, then, that Anne Hathaway Shakespeare was with child at the time of her wedding. On February 2, 1585, the records of the parish church in Stratford note the baptisms of "Hamnet & Judeth, sonne and daughter to William Shakspere."

SHAKESPEARE INSULTED

On September 20, 1592, Robert Greene's *A Groats-worth of witte, bought with a million of Repentance* was entered in the Stationers' Register. In this work Shakespeare was publicly insulted as "an upstart Crow, beautified with our ["gentlemen" playwrights usually identified as Marlowe, Nashe, and Lodge] feathers, that with Tygers hart wrapt in a Players hyde [a parody of a Shakespearean line in II *Henry VI*] supposes he is as well able to bombast out a blank verse as the best of you: and being an absolute Iohannes fac totum, is in his own conceit the only Shake-scene in a country." This statement asperses not only Shakespeare's art but intimates his lowly birth. (A "John factotum" is a servant or a man of all work.)

On April 18, 1593, Shakespeare's long erotic poem "Venus and Adonis" was entered for publication. Printed under the author's name, it was dedicated to the nineteen-year-old Henry Wriothesley, Earl of Southampton. Just over a year later—on May 9, 1594—another long erotic poem, "The Rape of Lucrece," was entered for publication. It also was printed under Shakespeare's name and was dedicated to the Earl of Southampton.

On December 26 and 27, 1594, payment was made to Shakespeare and others for performances at court by the Lord Chamberlain's servants.

For August 11, 1596, the parish register of Holy Trinity Church records the burial of "Hamnet filius William Shakspere."

FROM "VILLEIN" TO "GENTLEMAN"

On October 20, 1596, John Shakespeare, the poet's father, was made a "gentleman" by being granted the privilege of bearing a coat of arms. Thus, William Shakespeare on this day also became a "gentleman." Shakespeare's mother, Mary Arden Shakespeare, was "gentle" by birth. The poet was a product of a cross-class marriage. Both the father and the son were technically "villeins" or "villains" until this day.

On May 24, 1597, William Shakespeare purchased New Place, a large house in the center of Stratford.

CITED AS "BEST"

In 1598 Francis Meres's *Palladis Tamia* listed Shakespeare

more frequently than any other English author. Shakespeare was cited as one of eight by whom "the English tongue is mightily enriched, and gorgeouslie invested in rare ornaments and resplendent abiliments"; as one of six who had raised "monumentum aere perennius" [a monument more lasting than brass]; as one of five who excelled in lyric poetry; as one of thirteen "best for Tragedie," and as one of seventeen who were "best for Comedy."

On September 20, 1598, Shakespeare is said on the authority of Ben Jonson (in his collection of plays, 1616) to have been an actor in Jonson's *Every Man in His Humour.*

On September 8, 1601, the parish register of Holy Trinity in Stratford records the burial of "Mr. Johannes Shakespeare," the poet's father.

BECOMES A "KING'S MAN"

In 1603 Shakespeare was named, with others, as the Lord Chamberlain's players, as licensed by James I (Queen Elizabeth having died) to become the King's Men.

In 1603 a garbled and pirated *Hamlet* (now known as Q1) was printed with Shakespeare's name on the title page.

In March 1604, King James gave Shakespeare, as one of the Grooms of the Chamber (by virtue of being one of the King's Men), four yards of red cloth for a livery, this being in connection with a royal progress through the City of London.

In 1604 (probably) there appeared a second version of *Hamlet* (now known as Q2), enlarged and corrected, with Shakespeare's name on the title page.

On June 5, 1607, the parish register at Stratford records the marriage of "M. John Hall gentleman & Susanna Shaxspere," the poet's elder daughter. John Hall was a doctor of medicine.

BECOMES A GRANDFATHER

On February 21, 1608, the parish register at Holy Trinity, Stratford, records the baptism of Elizabeth Hall, Shakespeare's first grandchild. On September 9, 1608, the same parish register records the burial of Mary Shakespeare, the poet's mother.

On May 20, 1609, "Shakespeares Sonnets. Never before Imprinted" was entered for publication.

On February 10, 1616, the marriage of Judith, Shakespeare's younger daughter, is recorded in the parish register of Holy Trinity, Stratford.

On March 25, 1616, Shakespeare made his will. It is extant.

On April 23, 1916, Shakespeare died. The monument in the Stratford church is authority for the date.

BURIED IN STRATFORD CHURCH

On April 25, 1616, Shakespeare was buried in Holy Trinity Church, Stratford. Evidence of this date is found in the church register. A stone laid over his grave bears this inscription:

> Good Frend for Iesus Sake Forbeare, To Digg The Dust Encloased Heare! Blest Be The Man That Spares Thes Stones, And Curst Be He That Moves My Bones.

DEMAND FOR MORE INFORMATION

These are the life records of Shakespeare. Biographers of necessity flesh out these (and other) not very revealing notices from 1564-1616, Shakespeare's life span, with ancillary matter such as the status of Elizabethan actors, details of the Elizabethan theaters, and life under Elizabeth I and James I. Information about Shakespeare's artistic life—for example, his alteration of his sources—is much more abundant than truthful insights into his personal life, including his beliefs. There is, of course, great demand for colorful stories about

Shakespeare, and there is intense pressure on biographers to depict the poet as a paragon of wisdom.

ANECDOTES—TRUE OR UNTRUE?

Biographers of Shakespeare may include stories about Shakespeare that have been circulating since at least the seventeenth century; no one knows whether or not these stories are true. One declares that Shakespeare was an apprentice to a butcher, that he ran away from his master, and that he was received by actors in London. Another story holds that Shakespeare was, in his youth, a schoolmaster somewhere in the country. Another story has Shakespeare fleeing from his native town to escape the clutches of Sir Thomas Lucy, who had often had him whipped and sometimes imprisoned for poaching deer. Yet another story represents the youthful Shakespeare as holding horses and taking care of them while their owners attended the theater.

Scholarly and certainly lay expectations oblige Shakespearean biographers often to resort to speculation. This may be very well if biographers use such words as conjecture, presumably, seems, and almost certainly. For example, consider this example of hedged thought and language from Hazelton Spencer's *The Art and Life of William Shakespeare* (1940): "Of politics Shakespeare seems to have steered clear . . . but at least by implication Shakespeare reportedly endorses the strong-monarchy policy of the Tudors and Stuarts." Similarly, in David Shelley Berkeley's *Blood Will Tell in Shakespeare's Plays* (1984): "Shakespeare particularly faults his numerous villeins for lacking the classical virtue of courage (they are cowards) and for deficiencies in reasoning ability (they are 'fools'), and in speech (they commit malapropisms), for lack of charity, for ambition, for unsightly faces and poor physiques, for their smell, and for their harboring lice." This remark is not necessarily biographical or reflective of Shakespeare's personal beliefs; it refers to Shakespeare's art in that it makes general assertions about the base—those who lacked coats of arms—as they appear in the poet's thirty-seven plays. The remark's truth or lack of truth may be tested by examination of Shakespeare's writings.

WHO WROTE SHAKESPEARE'S PLAYS?

Some biographers of Shakespeare, including some of weighty names, state assumptions as if they were facts concerning the poet's beliefs. Perhaps the most egregious are those who cannot conceive that the Shakespearean plays were written by a person not a graduate of Oxford or Cambridge and destitute of the insights permitted by foreign travel and by life at court. Those of this persuasion insist that the seventeenth Earl of Oxford, Edward de Vere (whose descendant Charles Vere has spoken up for the Earl's authorship of the Shakespearean plays), or Sir Francis Bacon, or someone else wrote the Shakespearean plays. It is also argued that the stigma of publication would besmirch the honor of an Elizabethan aristocrat who published under his own name (unless he could pretend to correct a pirated printing of his writings).

BEN JONSON'S TESTIMONY

Suffice it here to say that the thought of anyone writing the plays and giving them to the world in the name of Shakespeare would have astonished Ben Jonson, a friend of the poet, who praised Shakespeare to the skies for his comedies and tragedies in the fine poem "To the Memory of My Beloved Master the Author, Mr. William Shakespeare, and What He Hath Left Us" (printed in the First Folio, 1623). Much more commonplace and therefore much more obtrusive upon the minds of Shakespeare students are those many scholars who are capable of writing, for example, that Shakespeare put more of himself into Hamlet than any of his other characters or that the poet had no rigid system of religion or morality. Even George Lyman Kittredge, the greatest American Shakespearean, wrote, "Hamlet's advice to the players has always been understood—and rightly—to embody Shakespeare's own views on the art of acting."

In point of fact, we know nothing of Shakespeare's beliefs or opinions except such obvious inferences as that he must have thought New Place, Stratford, worth buying because he bought it. Even Homer, a very self-effacing poet, differs in this matter from Shakespeare. Twice in the *Iliad* he speaks in his own voice (distinguished from the dialogue of his characters) about certain evil deeds of Achilles. Shakespeare left no letters, no diary, and no prefaces (not counting conventionally obsequious dedications); no Elizabethan Boswell tagged Shakespeare around London and the provinces to record his conversation and thus to reveal his mind. In his plays Shakespeare employed no rainsonneur, or authorial mouthpiece, as some other dramatists have done: contrary to many scholarly assertions, it cannot be proved that Prospero, in *The Tempest* in the speech ending "I'll drown my book" (Act V), and Ulysses, in *Troilus and Cressida* in the long speech on "degree" (Act II), speak Shakespeare's own sentiments. All characters in all Shakespearean plays speak for themselves. Whether they speak also for Shakespeare cannot be proved because documents outside the plays cannot be produced.

As for the sonnets, they have long been the happy hunting ground of biographical extremists who lack outside documents, who do not recognize that Shakespeare may have been using a persona, and who seem not to know that in Shakespeare's time good sonnets were supposed to read like confessions.

Some critics even go to the length of professing to hear Shakespeare speaking in the speech of a character and uttering his private beliefs. An example may be found in A. L. Rowse's *What Shakespeare Read and Thought* (1981): "Nor is it so difficult to know what Shakespeare thought or felt. A writer, Logan Pearsall Smith, had the perception to see that a personal tone of voice enters when Shakespeare is telling you what he thinks, sometimes almost a raised voice; it is more obvious again when he urges the same point over and over."

WHERE'S THE PROOF?

Rowse, deeply enamoured of his ability to hear Shakespeare's own thoughts in the speeches of characters speaking in character, published a volume entitled *Shakespeare's Self-Portrait, Passages from His Work* (1984). One critic might hear Shakespeare voicing his own thoughts in a speech in *Hamlet;* another might hear the author in *Macbeth.* Shakespearean writings can become a vast whispering gallery where Shakespeare himself is heard *hic et ubique* (here and everywhere), without an atom of documentary proof.

"BETTER SO"

Closer to truth is Matthew Arnold's poem on Shakespeare:

> Others abide our question. Thou art free.
> We ask and ask—thou smilest and art still,
> Out-topping knowledge. For the loftiest hill,
> Who to the stars uncrowns his majesty,
>
> Planting his steadfast footsteps in the sea,
> Making the heaven of heavens his dwelling-place,
> Spares but the cloudy border of his base
> To the foiled searching of mortality;
>
> And thou, who didst the stars and sunbeams know,
> Self-schooled, self-scanned, self-honoured, self-secure,
> Didst tread the earth unguessed at.—Better so. . . .

Here Arnold has Dichtung und Wahrheit—both poetry and truth—with at least two abatements: He exaggerates Shakespeare's wisdom (the poet, after all, is not God) and fails to acknowledge that Shakespeare's genius was variously recognized in his own time. Jonson, for example, recorded that the "players [actors of the poet's time] have often mentioned it as an honor to Shakespeare, that in his writing (whatsoever he penned) he never blotted a line" (Timber); and of course there is praise of Shakespeare, some of it quoted above, in Meres's *Palladis Tamia* (1598). And Germaine Greer, in *Shakespeare* (1986), concludes: "Shakespeare was not a propagandist; he did not write plays as vehicles for his own ideas. Rather he developed a theatre of dialectical conflict, in which idea is pitted against idea and from their friction a deeper understanding of the issues emerges."

THE BEST APPROACH

Hippocrates' first apothegm states, "Art is long, but life is short." Even King Solomon, speaking in Ecclesiastes, complained of too many books. One must be, certainly in our time, very selective. Shakespeare's ipsissima verba (his very words) should of course be studied, and some of them memorized. Then, if one has time, the golden insights of criticism from the eighteenth century to the present should be perused. (The problem is to find them all in one book!) And the vast repetitiousness, the jejune stating of the obvious, and the rampant subjectivity of much Shakespearean criticism should be shunned.

Then, if time serves, the primary sources of Shakespeare's era should be studied because the plays were not impervious to colorings imparted by the historical matrix. Finally, if the exigencies of life permit, biographers of Shakespeare who distinguish between fact and guesswork, such as Marchette Chute (Shakespeare of London), should be consulted. The happiest situation, pointed to by Jesus in Milton's *Paradise Regained,* is to bring judgment informed by knowledge to whatever one reads.

ROMEO AND JULIET
INTRODUCTION

For years the peace of Verona has been disturbed by the periodic feuding of two families, the Montagues and the Capulets, who bear an ancient grudge. At the start of the play, this feud is revived by some troublesome servants. That very evening the Capulets are holding a traditional family party. Romeo, a Montague, accidentally learns of the party, and decides to crash it with some of his friends. At the party, he sees and falls instantly in love with Juliet, Lord Capulet's daughter. She returns his love and, after the party, the young couple woo each other in Capulet's orchard. It is a short courtship; they agree to be secretly married the next day. Romeo then goes joyfully to see his priest, Friar Laurence, to arrange for the ceremony. He informs Juliet of the time and place by giving a message to her Nurse, and the couple meet and are married that very afternoon. It is arranged that Romeo shall come to Juliet's bedroom at nightfall.

Romeo impatiently passes the intervening hours with his friends, among them the swift-witted Mercutio. As they walk, Tybalt Capulet appears. Tybalt had seen Romeo at the Capulet party and, feeling this to be insulting, he challenges Romeo to a duel. But Romeo, in the transports of love, is unwilling to fight his new cousin. Mercutio fights in Romeo's place and is killed. This death is too much for Romeo. He begins to duel with Tybalt, kills him in turn, and flees to the safety of the Friar's cell. Verona's Prince declares Romeo's punishment to be exile. Beside themselves with misery at this new turn of events, the newlyweds spend their first and last night together and then part sadly. No sooner has Romeo left than grave news comes to Juliet: Her parents have arranged for her to marry a young gentleman named Paris. Unwilling to reveal her secret marriage and unable to dishonor herself and her love by agreeing to a second marriage, Juliet causes a huge family quarrel by refusing. When her father threatens to throw her out of the house if she does not change her mind, Juliet hurries to the Friar for advice.

The plan decided on is a desperate one: Juliet will pretend to consent to the marriage; but the night before the wedding, she will swallow a sleeping potion that will make her seem to be dead. Her parents and Paris will mourn for her and place her in the family vault. The Friar will inform Romeo, who will be beside Juliet when she awakens, to take her away with him. Juliet then goes home to her parents, carries off the deception, and takes the potion. The next morning, her official wedding day, she is discovered, believed dead, and mourned pitifully. So far, so good. But the Friar's message fails to reach Romeo. Instead, Romeo hears the news that his bride is dead—and determines to join her in death. He plans go to her tomb and kill himself there by taking poison. At the last minute the Friar discovers that his message has not been delivered, so he decides to go to the tomb and fetch Juliet himself.

Arriving at the tomb, Romeo meets Paris, who has come to mourn Juliet. Paris wishes to arrest Romeo for breaking his exile; in the ensuing fight, Romeo kills Paris. Romeo now enters the tomb, says his farewell to the sleeping Juliet, and takes the poison. Seconds after his death, the Friar arrives and Juliet awakes. The Friar cannot persuade the girl to leave her newly dead lover. He flees, and Juliet kills herself with Romeo's dagger. Again in a matter of seconds the guards arrive, find the three corpses, and sound the alarm. When the two feuding families and the Prince of Verona are assembled, the Friar comes forward and explains what has happened. His story is corroborated by a farewell letter Romeo has sent to his father. Seeing how the feud has brought such tragedy to the secret love of the two young people, the Capulets and the Montagues decide to call an end to their feud, and peace is restored to Verona.

SHAKESPEARE'S USE OF CONVENTION

Astrology played a large part in the lives of even the best educated Elizabethans. It was believed that there were four humours of the body: blood, phlegm, choler (yellow bile), and melancholy (black bile). These humours supposedly controlled a person's health and temperament. Only an even-tempered person had all these humours in the right proportions. If someone was limp and lacking in drive, it was believed that phlegm was the controlling humour: that is, he or she was phlegmatic. Tybalt, with his quick temper, would have been judged to be controlled by yellow bile, or choler. Examples could be given for predominance of any of the four humours. These humours, in turn, were believed to be responsive to the positions of the stars and planets. This was called the "influence" of the stars, and the effect can be compared to the effect the moon has on the tides of the ocean. The planet Mars, when in a certain position in relation to the sun and the signs of the zodiac, was believed to cause a response rising from the yellow bile, and a choleric individual such as Tybalt would be more easily angered at such a time. Thus the influence of the stars dominated daily life. Because it caused people to behave and react without knowing why, this influence was regarded as a kind of fate. Sometimes, upon the birth of a child, an astrologer would be called in to read the child's future, describe his temperament, and even chart out favorable and unfavorable years, months, and days. So we see that the description of Romeo and Juliet as "star-cross'd lovers" is not merely an image. From birth, their controlling stars and humours had marked them out for an unavoidable fate. Even their love, which seemed to spring up so naturally and quickly at first sight, may have been considered by the Elizabethans to be predetermined. Certainly, the love was fatal. This romantic love goes with death, it must end in death; and if the humours of the lovers cause them to choose this kind of love, they choose their death at the same time. Shakespeare used this kind of imagery often.

Another important convention in the play is that of courtly and romantic love. During the Middle Ages, the Church did much to shape views of love. Love was first to be given to God. Gradually there developed an entire posture of love, in an effort to reconcile earthly love with heavenly love. The woman who was the object of love became an object of worship and was adored as though she were the Virgin Mary. She became absolutized—a perfect celestial being—and to love her was the only means to ecstasy and sublime fulfillment. Yet such distance was not really desired by the lover. He prayed for her blessings, but by this he meant sexual favors. Thus romance entered the picture, and love became at once holy and profane. Secrecy and adultery were as significant a part of the emotion as religious transcendence. Courtly love was centered on this apparent contradiction, and the feeling that if the fruits of love were forbidden they became just so much more desirable. Still, much conflict arose out of the inherent paradox. In an attempt to reconcile profane love with the Church, such love was regarded as requiring service to the woman loved, and great civility and courtliness. The ideal end was heaven on earth in a woman's arms. Yet the conflicting aspects of this one emotion remained. Out of a need for balance these arose a contrary current of jest, bawdy songs, and lusty stories or fabliaux. The tendency was to react against the divinity of woman by reducing her to a more natural state—that of a mere means for satisfying fleshly appetites.

These tendencies are apparent in Romeo and Juliet. When Romeo believes himself in love with Rosaline, he assumes the postures made famous by Petrarch, an Italian author of numerous sonnets. Petrarch has sensed clearly enough the conflicts inherent in the position of a courtly lover. The expression of these emotions through opposites, or contradictories linked together, was typical of Petrarch; and Romeo, like every youth who wished to be in love, imitated these postures of adoration and melancholy that had become famous. (Northrop Frye calls Romeo's love affair with Rosaline "a kind of pedantry, like Tybalt's fighting by the book of arithmetic.") The impulse to pooh-pooh such ideals and attitudes as unnatural and funny finds expression in the mouths of both Mercutio and the Nurse. The love shared by Romeo and Juliet is another matter, however, for Shakespeare succeeded in achieving a total and natural synthesis of the conflicting tendencies of love. There is still all the excitement of secrecy characteristic of romantic love, but there is no adultery. The lovers are married. The love is wholly an earthly one, but the lovers approach it with a holy innocence and wonder and newness; they commit themselves to it as totally and faithfully as if it were a religion. Indeed, it is their religion, and the end of it is in eternity, beyond life and death. There is never a doubt that theirs is to be a complete marriage, of bodies and passions as well as souls and imaginations. Even the devout Friar takes this for granted, and it is assumed that holy matrimony is not completed until physical union, as well as union of the hearts and souls, is completed by the lovers.

In order to achieve this synthesis, and to make this love both the most real and unique, and the most ideal and universal of all loves, Shakespeare chooses to retain the forms of conventional love poetry and give them new life. The first is the sonnet that the lovers speak at their first meeting. In style, it is a Petrarchan sonnet, dealing with a familiar idea of courtly love, the prayer for a kiss. The earthly passion of the desire to kiss is balanced by the hallowed atmosphere of prayer and forgiveness of sin. The two tendencies that are so much a part of the Petrarchan lovers' posture are clear, but they are reconciled without strain. They do not seem in any way contrived or artificial. Juliet's invocation of her bridal night takes the form (except that there is no rhyme) of the epithalamium, a poem traditionally delivered before the consummation of marriage to celebrate the union of the couple. Her speech is a very passionate one, and the healthy honesty of this expression of passion makes the wedding poem both more pure and chaste—and more real than the more conventional poems of this sort. The parting dialogue between Romeo and Juliet also takes a traditional form: that of the "aubade" or dawn-song. The dawn-song always takes place at dawn between two lovers who have secretly spent the night together and who are torn between their desire to stay together and their fear of discovery. The conflict within them is traditionally expressed in a debate as to whether the light is the sun's or the moon's, whether that bird is a nightingale or a lark. The form gains new intensity, however, because we know that the feud has forced secrecy upon the lovers and that Romeo faces execution if he is not gone, undiscovered, from Verona in time. The dawn-song receives greater weight by the accumulating meaning of the imagery of light and dark, love and death, in the course of the play. Shakespeare has used conventional lyric forms and given them newness and life.

ROMEO AND JULIET
ACT I

PROLOGUE

The play opens with a sonnet spoken by a chorus. (Actually, the prologue probably was spoken by a single actor, the same actor who will speak the sonnet at the beginning of Act II.) These fourteen lines outline the action of the play and its effect upon the lives of the characters. In Verona, a pleasant Italian town, two equally important families that long have harbored grudges against each other break out into open feud. Romeo, son of the Montague family, and Juliet, daughter of the Capulet family, fall fatally in love; and only through their love and their death together can the long strife between the two families also die. This "death-mark'd" love is the subject of the play.

COMMENT

The device of an introductory chorus was used by Shakespeare in more than one play. It was an excellent way to set the scene and to capture the attention of the audience. The fact that in this case the prologue is a sonnet illustrates the formal, graceful rhetoric characteristic of Shakespeare at this time and of this play in particular. The chorus makes clear what will happen in the play, but not how it will happen. To find that out, you are asked to have the patience to listen to the actors present their play. That it will end in tragedy is sure, because of such words as "star-cross'd" and "death-mark'd." This is one of the relatively few premonitions in the play.

ACT I, SCENE 1

Sampson and Gregory, two of Capulet's servants, armed because of the long-standing feud, are joking with each other as they walk in Verona. Sampson declares that he will "not carry coals," that being the work of laborers. He means that he will not submit to being humiliated by the servants of Montague. Gregory retorts that if they did carry coals, they would be colliers, and colliers had the reputation of being dirty and of cheating. Sampson returns the pun so as to clarify his meaning: If "we be in choler [anger], we'll draw [swords]." Gregory continues to banter, deliberately misunderstanding Sampson and implying that he is a coward who is slow to draw his sword and quick to run when faced with danger. Sampson enjoys being teased and finally gets the upper hand by announcing that he will either cut off the heads of the maidens of Montague, "or their maidenheads, take it in what sense thou wilt." Gregory quibbles and the two exchange a few more bawdy jokes—until they find themselves actually drawing swords, because Abraham and Balthasar, servants of the Montague family, appear.

COMMENT

Here are two typical clowns, whose ribald wit and humor is intended to catch your interest and make you laugh. Shakespeare often enjoyed puns, or plays on words, such as those Sampson and Gregory make.

Two other points warrant attention here. First, the feeling of emergency is sensed immediately. The servants are armed; furthermore, their conversation, for all its joking, is concerned directly with the feud and the need for courage on their part. Perhaps they are whistling in the dark, or making jokes because they really do feel something ominous. Sampson's threats sound like empty boasting. Secondly, the sexual content of the jokes and boasts establishes one of the themes, later to be taken up by Mercutio and by Juliet's Nurse, and by the whole play. The important aspect here is that love is treated as simply lowlife sex, although with real warmth and gusto.

Facing the Montague family servants with drawn swords, Sampson and Gregory continue to joke with each other, but more furtively. Sampson again makes a phallic reference by saying "My naked weapon is out," and Gregory still implies that Sampson will run away with fright. Yet it is Sampson who takes up the challenge and shows his bravado first by provoking a fight. At this moment Gregory, who has been urging the fight, sees Tybalt, a Capulet, coming, and tells Sampson to assert that his master is better. What Gregory has not seen is Benvolio, a Montague, coming from the opposite direction. The four servants draw swords and begin to fight.

COMMENT

The tension mounts during this short scene, and it becomes clear that the feud is real, that both sides are looking for a fight, and that all assume a bravado that will lead inevitably to a renewed feud.

Coming quickly upon the fighting servants, Benvolio tries to stop them, saying, "Put up your swords; you know not what you do." But Tybalt, seeing Benvolio with his sword unsheathed, derides him for fighting among cowardly menials. Although Benvolio wants only to stop the fight and "keep the peace," Tybalt is furious; he declares that he hates peace as much as he hates hell and the Montagues. As Benvolio and Tybalt fall to fighting, they are joined by more Capulets and Montagues. The sound of clashing swords is joined by the clubs of Officers of the Peace, who call for the downfall of both the feuding houses that disturb Verona's peace.

COMMENT

The difference between the characters of Tybalt and Benvolio is very clear. To Benvolio, fighting is caused by ignorance, and those who fight do not realize the consequences of violence. Wanting only to have peace between the two families, he is dismayed at this sense-less renewal of the feud. Tybalt is far more impetuous. He uses the word 'hate' twice, and 'death' once. He wants to kill, and to him this cold war between the families can only end in drawn swords. Ironically, through the joking of the servants the feud has begun again.

Lord Capulet and Lord Montague now come on the scene. Both are eager to join the fight but are restrained by their wives. It is only when Escalus, Prince of Verona, arrives with his followers that fighting ceases. Prince Escalus scolds both families bitterly, calling them "enemies to peace" and there-fore "beasts," who have three times broken the peace of their town and its people, making even the aged take sides. He declares that the penalty for another fight shall be death.

COMMENT

The uppermost feeling in the minds of the townspeople, the audience, and even the wives of Capulet and Montague, is that peace, not war, is desirable. Through-out the play peace is desired by the two major charac-ters, but peace is finally won only through death. Prince Escalus speaks not only for the town but for the whole play when he suggests that if nothing else stops the feud, it will be ended by making death the punishment for it.

Only Lord and Lady Montague and Benvolio remain as the others depart. Benvolio again explains how the feud began; Lady Montague, however, is more concerned about her son, Romeo, whom she has not seen that day. Benvolio did see him, walking at dawn without company and clearly prefer-ring to be left alone. Montague comments that Romeo has been in such a mood for quite awhile—weeping and moon-ing, staying out all night but going in as soon as the sun rises, locking himself in his room with the curtains drawn as if to make "himself an artificial night." Montague tells Benvolio that he does not know the cause, but "would as willingly give cure as know." At this point they see Romeo coming, so Benvolio tells the Lord and Lady to "step aside" while he attempts to find out what is bothering Romeo.

COMMENT

This description of Romeo is a stereotype of the romantic lover of Shakespeare's time. He keeps to the darkness and the night, he writes poetry, and he revels in sorrow, tears, secrecy, and being alone. The audience probably would recognize Romeo's "affections" or attitudes instantly.

Yes, Romeo is in love, but the lady does not "favour" him, so he mourns, and the hours seem long. Romeo would like to change the subject away from Benvolio's questions, but when Benvolio presses him, he pours out his heart in a series of paradoxes: "O brawling love! O loving hate! . . . O heavy lightness! O serious vanity!/ Misshapen chaos of well-seeming forms!/ Feather of lead, bright smoke, cold fire, sick health!" Romeo feels miserable and forlorn, and he tells Benvolio that he accepts this change in himself as part of love: "This is not Romeo, he's some other where." He loves a woman who does not love him and who insists on remaining chaste. Romeo refuses to say who she is. Benvolio suggests that Romeo try to forget her and begin looking at other pretty girls, but the young lover insists that he cannot, that such a thing is impossible. They leave, and Benvolio goes to report to Lord Montague.

COMMENT

Romeo's description of his feeling is important, for it confirms an Elizabethan stereotype. Romeo uses all the conceits or artificial conceptions about the feeling of love that were current in Elizabethan England. He has replaced life with literature, and he has assumed the artificial poses of love in a book. His speech is in rhymed couplets, or pairs of lines, which are not commonly found in Shakespeare's blank verse. The use of such couplets indicates that Shakespeare intends Romeo's language to be considered flowery and ornamental, and that we can take Romeo's protestations a little less than seriously.

Romeo describes love with all the conventionally contradictory words (such as "bright smoke, cold fire") that were used in love sonnets at that time. His beloved is beautiful, but remote and cruel, for she refuses to show her feelings or give up her chastity.

This is significant because Romeo has not met Juliet; he thinks he loves Rosaline, who is also a Capulet. His artificial feelings later will be contrasted with real ones. The true emotions may find expression in contradictions, but they will be genuinely felt. They also will be involved with the meaning and imagery of the play rather than remaining distant and literary, as these are. Romeo says he is not himself; indeed, he becomes his true self only when he finds Juliet.

SUMMARY

The action of the play has begun, and three main themes can be seen:

(1) The feud between the Capulets and the Montagues has started again because of servants spoiling for a fight. The fact that such seemingly insignificant people could start the feud again gives us a feeling that the feud is fated to take place and can lead only to disaster and death before it runs its course. Even Benvolio's efforts are lost because of the rashness of Tybalt. The impetuosity and speed of the action strengthen our feeling that fate will become important in our understanding of the play.

(2) An omen of death hangs heavy in the air. Tybalt has spoken of hate, and Prince Escalus has made death the penalty for fighting. We begin to think that, despite everything, the feud can end only through death.

(3) At the same time, there has been much talk of love. The servants speak of bawdy sexual love. Romeo has illustrated an elevated, artificial, literary love. Clearly, love in all its aspects will be a major theme.

We have met Lords Capulet and Montague, heads of the two feuding households. Also introduced was Prince Escalus, governor of Verona. These are the three leaders, but not the main characters. Formality is a keynote here; it will be seen again later in the occupation with such social customs as invitations to a party and formal proposals of marriage. Formality of structure appears both in the language and in the very idea of a feud that divides the play and its characters into opposing parties. We have sampled various important styles of language, such as the coarse humor of servants (who do not speak in blank verse) and the flowery rhetoric of Romeo. All this will be developed further.

ACT I, SCENE 2

Having met the Montagues, we now meet Lord Capulet, walking through Verona's streets with Paris, a relative of Prince Escalus. They are returning from visiting the Prince, and as they walk they discuss the recently imposed penalty for further feuding. Capulet feels that men of their age should be able to keep peace. Paris agrees, but soon turns the conversation to a matter closer to his heart: his wish to marry Capulet's fourteen-year-old daughter, Juliet. They have discussed the suit of marriage before, and Capulet maintains that she is yet too young. He urges Paris to wait two years, when she will be "ripe to be a bride." Capulet hesitates. His words reveal that he loves his daughter deeply and has placed all his remaining hope on earth in her. Still, he favors the marriage; and if Paris can win Juliet's consent, Capulet will not oppose it. He invites Paris to a party to be held at his house that evening. At the party will be many pretty young girls, "Earth-treading stars that make dark heaven light," and Lord Capulet would have Paris see them all in comparison with Juliet before he makes up his mind.

COMMENT

This is the first we hear of Juliet, and it is not surprising that we hear of her in the context of love and peace.

Capulet and Paris, an old man and a young one, both come from the freshly renewed feud. But they hope that age with its wisdom will further the cause of peace. Paris is in love with Juliet. That Capulet also loves her is clear, for he dotes on her, even allowing her to have the final word about whether to marry. (Traditionally, marriages between members of aristocratic families were arranged by the parents.) Just as Capulet, in his old age, hopes for peace, he puts his hope for life in his daughter. He is shown to be a dignified old man and an indulgent father.

Besides the theme of love and peace, we have here clearly described the contrast between youth and age. That contrast is illustrated by the conversation between the old father and the young lover, and it later becomes thematic.

Capulet has given to one of his servants a list of people whom the servant is to see are invited to his party. The servant cannot read the list, however, and after puzzling over it a bit, he stops two strangers in the street and asks them to read it to him. The strangers are none other than Romeo and Benvolio, still discussing Romeo's lovesick state and what to do about it. Benvolio again tells his friend, in a series of images, that a new love affair alone will cure old lovesickness. Again Romeo tries to turn the conversation and, in the next breath, bewails his state. The servant then interrupts and Romeo, after jesting with him, reads the list of guests to be invited (as the servant reveals) to Capulet's party that evening. The servant adds, before departing, that if they are not Montagues, they surely will be welcome. One of the guests whose name Romeo read out was the fair Rosaline.

COMMENT

This adds a new twist to the plot. It is not strange that the servant cannot read, as few of that class were literate. It would be natural for him to stop two aristocrats on the street, ask them to read the list, and then hospitably extend the invitation to them. But it is chance, and seems like fate, that these two aristocrats are both Montagues, and one is Romeo. Again, as in the renewal of the feud, the intervention of what appears to be accident has forced the action in the direction designated by the prologue. Along with the importance of being literary, and of such formalities of life as invitations and hospitality, we are struck by a larger, more fateful force on the action.

Romeo and Benvolio promptly decide to "crash" the party. Doing so suits the purposes of both. Kindly Benvolio sees it as a chance for Romeo to compare Rosaline with other young ladies. He hopes that she will not withstand the comparison, and that this romance will give way to a new one. Of course, Romeo protests fervently, again claiming that this could never be. His language is loaded with contraries and comparisons of his love to religion. But he would be happy to go, just to see Rosaline. Romeo and Benvolio depart.

COMMENT

Romeo is still in love with love, speaking of it as a religion, a comparison derived from courtly love traditions. (See Introduction.) Benvolio is still gentle, considerate, and sincerely intent on helping Romeo with good advice. The characters have not changed; nevertheless, chance, or fate, and the impulsiveness of youth, are taking them to a party at the house of their enemy, on the very evening of the renewed feud.

SUMMARY

This scene has done much to further the exposition of the play; that is, it has furthered the action by introducing another set of possibilities. Paris is officially courting Juliet and is to make his decision tonight at Capulet's party. Romeo is to go to his enemy's traditional celebration, to see Rosaline or to begin to forget her. Although neither the audience nor the characters know it, the party will be of vital importance, for there Romeo will meet Juliet. The exposition also serves to introduce more characters: in this case, not only Lord Capulet and Paris, but by reference, Juliet herself. We have seen more of Romeo's posturing, of Benvolio's steadfastness, and of the formalism and the power of fate that characterize the play.

ACT I, SCENE 3

The scene changes now from Verona's streets to the house of the Capulets, where Lady Capulet is telling the old Nurse to call Juliet. The Nurse swears by the purity she had when she was a twelve-year-old that she has called Juliet, and calls again. Juliet comes, obediently. Lady Capulet has something to tell her daughter, and at first tells the Nurse to go; but then she lets her stay, for the Nurse has known Juliet since birth. The mere reference to how long she has known Juliet starts the Nurse onto a string of repetitive memories that both mother and daughter are hard put to bring to a halt. The Nurse knows Juliet's age to the day (two weeks younger than fourteen years), because her own daughter, Susan, was born on the same day and died soon after. Because of these circumstances she had become Juliet's wet nurse, which she remained for three years, until the earthquake. Rambling through her memories, the Nurse remembers the very day when Juliet was weaned from her milk. (This was accomplished, as was the custom in Elizabethan times, by rubbing wormwood, a bitter herb, on the breast. From this the child recoiled.) Even the day before the weaning, the Nurse remembers Juliet had been able to walk by herself, had fallen, and bumped her head. The Nurse's husband had picked up the crying child and jokingly said, "Dost thou fall upon thy face?/ Thou wilt fall backward when thou has more wit." At this colorful reference to her own yet far-distant puberty, the baby had stopped crying, as though she had understood and agreed. The Nurse, delighted at the old joke, especially as Juliet is now of age, repeats it twice, with vigor and laughter. She relishes all the details and the appropriateness of the sexual reference. She is enjoying herself so well, that not until Juliet has reminded her does she begin to run down, only adding that she wants to see Juliet married once.

COMMENT

While we have met Juliet, we as yet know no more of her than that she is a docile young girl. Our chief interest in this passage is commanded by the Nurse. She is a wonderfully talkative older woman, whose language is abundant, colorful, and fully realized. Only she could speak these lines, and we become concretely aware of her character as much from her manner of speaking as from what she says. She is funny, gross, and delights in both humor and sex. The content of her speech here stands in direct contrast with the demure attitude of Juliet to follow; and her interest in seeing Juliet married is so that Juliet, too, may enjoy sex as the Nurse has done. Through this scene, we come to understand Juliet much better. As Northrop Frye explains: "We suddenly get a vision of what Juliet's childhood must have been like, wandering around a big house where her father is 'Sir' and her mother is 'Madam,' where to leave she must get special permission, not ordinarily granted except for visits to a priest for confession, and where she is waiting for the day when Capulet will say to his wife, in effect, 'I'm sure we've got a daughter around this place somewhere: isn't it time we got rid of her?'"

Marriage is indeed the subject that Lady Capulet has called Juliet to discuss, and she promptly asks her daughter how she feels about marrying. Juliet replies, "It is an honour that I dream not of." The Nurse, from her own point of view, praises Juliet for that answer, saying marriage is definitely an honor. Lady Capulet takes Juliet's reply as it was meant, with the emphasis on the word "dream," and encourages her to think about marriage, as Paris wishes to marry her. Both the Lady and the Nurse consider Paris a flower of manhood, and Lady Capulet launches into a long rhymed speech, comparing Paris to a book that is beautiful to see and to read, and that lacks only a binding—that is, a wife. She wants Juliet to see him at their party this very evening, and she urges Juliet to consider marrying him. Juliet answers, "I'll look to like, if looking liking move." When a servant comes to announce that the party is about to begin without them, the scene ends.

COMMENT

Lady Capulet, as a distinct contrast to the Nurse (whose whole view of love is natural), presents Paris as a possible husband in a wholly artificial way. She uses elaborate and ingenious conceits expanding on the metaphor "Read o'er the volume of young Paris' face." Our picture of her is of a literate lady of society who stresses manners and expresses herself in a correspondingly formal and artificial way. It almost seems as if she takes marriage lightly, although she clearly wants this one to take place. Juliet speaks only in response; her responses indicate a shy, sweet, innocent girl, young and docile, yet more humbled at the thought of love than she is to her mother's will. (See the above quotations.) Germaine Greer finds this a telling scene, noting the marked age difference between Lord and Lady Capulet and concluding, "Juliet's youth, and the general distortion of mores in a society which married children to old men, is an important aspect of the tragedy. In devoting herself to Romeo Juliet takes an irrevocably tragic step [for] she has to teach him the accepts of true love. . . ."

SUMMARY

The theme of this entire scene is love and marriage, and three distinct viewpoints have been presented:

(1) The humility and wonder of Juliet, an untried young girl, is the simplest.

(2) Lady Capulet approaches marriage as a worldly transaction: "So shall you share all that he doth possess,/ By having him making yourself no less." This is not cold of her; it was often the attitude among parents who arranged marriages for their children. A sense of the need of a moral core in a husband shows in her words "Tis much pride/ For fair without the fair within to hide." Still, her sense of love itself seems to be somewhat superficial, a matter for pretty speeches.

(3) As opposed to the more artificial view of Juliet's mother, her Nurse's view is natural. Love can be almost equated with lust, and both are matters for pleasure and fun. To Lady Capulet's remark that Juliet will be no less for marrying Paris, she retorts, "No less! nay, bigger; women grow by men." Marriage means sex, and sex means pregnancy, when women grow bigger. For the Nurse it is all as simple, natural, and enjoyable as that.

The introduction of Juliet has been made; and if she is only a slip of a girl as yet, our idea of her is rounded out and humanized by the Nurse's speeches, which run, full circle, from birth through weaning, puberty, and marriage, to pregnancy. The contrasted Nurse and mother probably were the formative influences on Juliet.

ACT I, SCENE 4

Romeo and Benvolio, along with a retinue of masked entertainers and torchbearers, are on their way through Verona's streets to Lord Capulet's party. With them is Mercutio, who is objective, as he is not a member of either of the feuding families, but is a relative of the Prince. He is also Romeo's close friend and confidant. It was traditional that masked gatecrashers should deliver a humorous "apology" for their intrusion, but to Romeo's question about what their apology shall be,

Benvolio replies that there should be none: "Let them measure us by what they will,/ We'll measure them a measure [dance out a formal dance pattern], and be gone." Benvolio prefers to overlook such usual frivolities, perhaps because they are going among enemies. Romeo, still keeping his lovesick attitude, declares that he does not even want to dance; he would rather carry a torch, as torchbearers do not dance. Mercutio chides him and Romeo replies with wit, though still on the same theme, that the "soles" of others' shoes are light for dancing, but his "soul" is too heavy. Mercutio again prods him; extending his wit with words still further, Romeo continues to protest that he is so "bound" by love that he cannot "bound"—that is, jump and dance about, or rise above the boundaries of ordinary conduct. When Mercutio comments that at this rate, Romeo will be such a burden on love that it will be crushed, Romeo retorts that love is not tender, but rough, and "it pricks like thorn." Mercutio crowns the wordplay by advising that if Romeo would treat love as it treats him, he'd have the better of it.

COMMENT

Despite Romeo's posturing as a sad lover, we see him here in a playful exchange of sophisticated witticisms with Mercutio. This is their accustomed manner together: light-hearted, worldly men-about-town who delight in testing their skill with words against each other. Although Romeo still claims that he is suffering, he enjoys the jesting, and the other side of his nature shows through. Mercutio is totally at home in this atmosphere; and while he is concerned for his friend's being unhappy, he is skeptical about what strikes him as sentimental, and he wishes that Romeo would come out of it.

Mercutio, for one, is exhilarated at the prospect of the party. Although he has been invited (as we know from hearing his name read off the servant's list; see scene 2 of this act), he calls for a mask; but then he decides that his face is ugly

enough to serve as a mask, and he puts the real one aside.
Romeo still wants a torch so that he won't have to dance, and
instead can give over the game and be a spectator. "Dun's the
mouse" ("Keep still") replies Mercutio, and again takes up the
game by teasing Romeo for being a stick-in-the-mud. But the
raillery slows, for Romeo has had a foreboding dream.

COMMENT

That Mercutio truly cares for Romeo is made still clearer
here by his efforts to rouse his friend and draw him fully
into the festival feeling. He jokes, not without some
deliberate meaning, about his own ugly face. He urges
Romeo to take the "good meaning" (that is, the encour-
agement from his words), and we shall see in the next
speech that he does not really brush off Romeo's
mention of a bad dream.

At Romeo's mention of a dream, Mercutio launches into an
extended (forty-two lines) speech of great fantasy and virtu-
osity, beginning with, "O, then I see Queen Mab hath been
with you." It is a real flight of the imagination, and is
well-known as the "Queen Mab speech." He calls Queen Mab
"the fairies' midwife," and describes her as being as small as a
figure carved in the stone of a ring. She comes in a cart made
of an empty hazelnut, fitted with parts made of grasshopper
wings, spider webs, and moonbeams, and drawn by tiny
creatures across the bridges of sleepers' noses. When she rides
through the brains of a lover, dreams of love result. She visits
all sorts of people, and those she visits dream that night of
their greatest desires or of the chief occupation of their life.
Nor are they all good dreams. Queen Mab is mischievous,
and sometimes she puts knots in horses' manes, a bad omen.
She does much, and all that she does is fabulous. Mercutio is
cut short by Romeo, who says, "Thou talk'st of nothing."
Mercutio assents, "True, I talk of dreams,/ Which are the
children of an idle brain,/ Begot of nothing but vain fantasy,/
Which is as thin a substance as the air,/ And more inconstant

than the wind." Benvolio reminds them that they are making themselves late to the party. Before they leave, however, Romeo adds that for him, they will not be too late, but too early, for he is still filled with premonitions of something about to happen that will result in his death.

COMMENT

Mercutio's wonderful speech, while it is perhaps irrelevant to the play in subject matter, is very important.

(1) It is a totally high-spirited, absurd product of imagination. A rare, fragile fantasy, full of delicacy and speed, beautiful sounds and images. Just this lightness and extravagance would be enough to win Mercutio to our hearts. The strength of our feeling for him later will play an important part when the tragic action of the play begins with his death.

(2) On another level, the Queen Mab speech is not so light. It modulates from a sheer conjuring trick into far more real images of soldiers starting awake as if fresh from battle and of women taught to bear the weight of men and children. Mercutio wholly delivers himself to the speech, and the changing tone illustrates both his desire to free his friend Romeo's mind of the omens of a bad dream and his deep perception of (and sympathy with) the effect of such a dream. It reveals Mercutio as a person who understands people well and who is a true friend to Romeo. The depth of this friendship is also focal in the tragedy to follow.

(3) Still keeping his light tone, Mercutio brushes off his Queen Mab speech in the last quotation above. But there is some bitterness at himself here. He says he speaks of dreams, and by that he means that Queen Mab herself is but a dream, emerged from his own "idle brain." He says that what we know to be the product of his genius

is born out of nothing, that it is "vain fantasy" and "inconstant." He is not only skeptical but disillusioned at what he feels is hollowness within himself. This self-deprecation and examination, this bitterness in such a seemingly light-hearted good fellow, allows us to understand his cynicism; it also cements our feeling about him.

The Queen Mab speech has been used to speed up the mood, but Romeo's foreboding continues too strongly; before he leaves, he says, "My mind misgives/ Some consequence, yet hanging in the stars,/ Shall bitterly begin his fearful date/ With this night's revels, and expire the term/ Of a despised life closed in my breast/ By some vile forfeit of untimely death." This is a crucial speech. It is not spoken in the conceits we have come to associate with Romeo's attitude of love. Indeed, it is a real premonition, for at this festival he meets Juliet, and their love leads directly to their deaths. It is "hanging in the stars," as foretold in the prologue's reference to "star-crossed lovers." (See the discussion of the influence of stars in the Introduction.) Stars are also significant later in the love imagery that Romeo and Juliet will share. The very quality of Romeo and Juliet's love contains its own destruction, and in that sense is fated to end in untimely death.

SUMMARY
Established in this scene were the following:

(1) Romeo is a brilliantly amusing young man, when he is not musing over his love. His friends enjoy him for his vivacity and worldly wit.

(2) Mercutio, a still more brilliant wit, and a more skeptical one than Romeo, is a deep friend of his, one of true feeling as well as wonderful fancy.

(3) Romeo's introspection has led to a very real feeling of some evil occurrence to come, and we share with him.

(4) The theme of sleep, which becomes an important one to the lovers, is introduced as the cause for Romeo's feeling of ill-omen and fate and as the subject for Mercutio's wild fantasy. Sleep has many aspects, and Shakespeare recognized it as a source for many of humanity's feelings and desires. Later, sleep becomes the object of desire, as it is the only time when parted lovers can find happiness.

ACT I, SCENE 5

After two scenes of preparation, we have come to the party at Lord Capulet's. We must remember that Romeo is here to see Rosaline, and Juliet to consider Paris as a future husband. The scene opens with bustling servants, cheerily fetching and carrying, calling to each other and cursing each other good-naturedly as they complete preparations for the party. As the servants go off, Lord Capulet with Juliet and his household comes to meet the entering guests and the maskers, Romeo among them. Capulet is in a jovial mood as host, a role he clearly enjoys. He threatens to accuse any lady who does not dance of having corns, and he remembers with the men the last time he came masked to parties and courted ladies. He calls for music, which is struck up, and merrily gives orders to the servants. Again, he comments on the unexpected fun of maskers and wonders with a cousin at the years passed since they played at such a role. This talk of maskers brings our attention to Romeo, who, amidst the gaiety, has called a servant apart from the crowd. He now asks, in a hushed voice, "What lady is that?" The lady is Juliet, whom he sees across the hall; and although the servant cannot answer his question and the room between them is alive with activity, it is as though no one else were in the room besides the two of them. He stands apart, rapturously praising her: "O, she doth teach the torches to burn bright. . . . Beauty too rich for use, for earth too dear." His speech is simple but full of graceful images; and in one word, he foreswears any love he has ever felt before.

COMMENT

This scene, when correctly staged, makes the audience feel that already Romeo and Juliet are alone in a crowd, and this will be essentially true throughout the rest of the play. Romeo's rhymed speech has now dropped all conceits and is true to feeling. His images of her, as a jewel in the ear of an Ethiopian and as a dove among crows, are strong. They place her in the context of whiteness, purity, and light amidst darkness. These images will remain central to our understanding of their love. Instantly, he forgets all courtly love, and feels the real thing.

Tybalt overhears Romeo speaking and becomes immediately furious at hearing a Montague's voice. He calls for his sword, and—inventing the excuse that Romeo has come to scorn the traditional Capulet feast—prepares to fight. He is restrained by Capulet himself, who was chastized by the Prince just that morning for feuding, and who now prefers peace. Besides, Capulet is the host, and he does not want his hospitality marred. Forcefully stating, "It is my will," and "He shall be endured," Capulet flies into a small temper himself, even calling Tybalt "a saucy boy," only to be distracted away by his duties to his guests. Tybalt, fuming at having to be patient, and promising that Romeo's intrusion will end bitterly, retreats.

COMMENT

Tybalt has shown his colors again as a rash, ill-tempered antagonist. He relents only when Capulet threatens him, saying, "I'll make you quiet." But Tybalt has not given up, and he promises to harbor a grudge that will play no small part in the action. Capulet, host at his own party, is feeling beneficent and generous. His response to the presence of a Montague is indulgent, and he voices praises he has heard on Romeo's behalf. He is in such a genial mood that only a disruption of his party can put him out of temper, and that not for long. But the flare-up of both characters indicates how close emotions are to the surface, even at a pleasant party.

In the commotion, Romeo has stolen across the room to where Juliet stands, and the two are alone together at one side of the hubbub. There is a precious silence around and between them. Romeo removes his mask and steps toward her. Their first words to each other form a sonnet. In his previous speech about her, Romeo hoped to touch Juliet's hand, and so bless his own hand. Now he says, "If I profane with my unworthiest hand/ This holy shrine." His lips, "two blushing pilgrims," he offers, as a gentler sin than the touch of his rough hand; but Juliet replies, "Good pilgrim, you do wrong your hand too much," and with natural sweetness she tells Romeo that saints and pilgrims kiss by clasping hands. (It is stage tradition that Romeo's masking costume is that of a pilgrim.) If hands kiss, then Romeo's lips will pray, and he prays for a kiss to purge his sin. They kiss, and the feeling between them is so strong that Juliet's only defense against her own heart is to remark, lightly and playfully, "You kiss by the book." The Nurse interrupts them to tell Juliet she is wanted by her mother.

COMMENT

Shakespeare often intensifies emotional effect by changes of pace and contrasts of setting. Here he has done both admirably. Action has been fast since the Queen Mab speech, and now the two lovers meet in the middle of hilarious gaiety and activity. Also, anger and the presence of the feud have made themselves felt just preceding this first expression of love. To further set apart the two lovers, they speak a sonnet. Their meeting is a meeting of two very young people, shy, sweet, and serious. The images of their first exchange of words are those of religion: Romeo calls Juliet a "holy shrine"; they speak of devotion, pilgrims, saints, prayer, and sin. It is no ordinary case of love at first sight, but a holy sacrament, hushed and sacred.

Juliet having gone to her mother, Romeo takes the opportunity to ask the Nurse who her mother is. The reply—that she is Lady Capulet—so astounds Romeo that he cannot answer before the Nurse adds her humorously pedestrian comment that whoever marries Juliet will be a rich man. Romeo responds starkly, "My life is my foe's debt." Already Romeo feels he would die without Juliet, and so he is in debt for his life to a family enemy. Benvolio, probably noticing his friend's agitation, urges that they leave; but as he is herding Romeo out, they are stopped by the hospitable Capulet, offering them food. This they refuse. As they depart, the party ends, and Capulet, satisfied, heads for bed.

COMMENT

Romeo has had to face the hardest blow that could possibly be dealt him, and he has met it squarely, accepting in one bare sentence all the difficulties it places on him. His sudden love is so real that, in moments, he has matured enough to say what would never have been expected of him before. He speaks in a paradox, but this one is charged with bitter meaning and acceptance of a burden beyond his previous experience.

Juliet, returning as the guests depart, is more subtle about finding out Romeo's identity. She asks her Nurse the names of several departing guests before she asks Romeo's. As her Nurse goes to find out who he is, she comments to herself, "If he be Married,/ My grave is like to be my wedding bed." She, too, feels that separation from this new-found lover would be her death. Her Nurse returns with far worse news—that he is a Montague—to which Juliet responds, as bravely and as stricken as Romeo, "My only love sprung from my only hate!" When her Nurse asks her what she is telling herself, she covers it up, saying it is only a rhyme she has just learned. The guests have all gone, and Juliet and the Nurse retire.

COMMENT

Already, as in Romeo's case, Juliet is gaining in maturity. She has fallen in love as deeply as he, and, as with Romeo, separation seems like death. She, too, sees a paradox in the ironic fate of loving an enemy. Her growing sophistication shows also in the means by which she twice, by slight deceptions, hides from the Nurse her true feelings. The emotion of love is bringing out the womanliness within the young girl.

For those who know the play, Juliet's equating of her wedding bed and her grave have added power. During the tragic course of the play, her wedding bed actually does become her grave. It is an excellent example of dramatic irony—a twisting of the audience's emotions when they know a meaning for words of which the speaker is not aware, and a device that Shakespeare frequently used.

SUMMARY

In the tumult of a party, and reminded by Tybalt's outburst of the feud between the houses, the two lovers have met.

(1) Their meeting is alone in a crowd and is sanctified by an air of holiness. The treatment of love as a religion was an integral part of the courtly love tradition (see the Introduction), but Shakespeare uses it in no ordinary way. Love is holy here; not even Friar Laurence, the servant of God, will put this love in tension against the love of God, as was part of the courtly love custom. Shakespeare wishes to unify earthly and celestial love and to give this love affair the attributes of both. The sacredness of Romeo and Juliet's passion will be emphasized throughout the play.

(2) The doom the lovers face is impressed on the audience by Tybalt's fury and by two separate realizations. Both Romeo and Juliet face fully the desperate reality of their situation without trying to hide or disguise it from themselves. In this, love has acted as a maturing force, changing them from childhood abruptly. The fore-doomed atmosphere is enhanced by the nature and degree of their love and by the impetuous rapidity of their falling into love.

ROMEO AND JULIET
ACT II

CHORUS

The chorus, like the prologue, is a sonnet. The two poems probably were both spoken by the same actor. Here, the important events of the first act are reiterated. Rosaline did not stand as beautiful in comparison with Juliet, and a new affection has replaced the old desire in Romeo's heart. But now, when both Romeo and Juliet are in love, they are prevented from natural courtship by the feud between their families. Only because their passion is so strong will they find the strength and means to carry on their secret courting.

COMMENT

This chorus is straightforward. By both reviewing the past and envisioning the future, it provides a transition for Romeo's abrupt change of heart. What is to come will be none too easy, but there is still a promise of joy for the lovers.

ACT II, SCENE 1

Romeo, fresh from meeting Juliet at Capulet's party, has ducked away from his comrades in search of solitude in which to contemplate this new state of events. Passing Capulet's orchard, he cannot find heart to take final leave of Juliet's house quite yet. It is as though he were made of the same earth as the orchard, and that earth were recalling him. He jumps over the wall, and fast on his heels come Mercutio and Benvolio, in search of him. Instead of continuing to call Romeo, Mercutio tries to conjure him up like a ghost from the grave. First he invokes Romeo by the image of his love-sickness: sighs, rhymes, and Cupid. When this brings no response, he tries by conjuring an image of Rosaline, whom he supposes, naturally enough, that Romeo still loves. Even playfully sensual images bring no angry stirring in the bushes. Benvolio relents, remarking that since Romeo is blind with love, dark fits him best, and they had best leave him alone. Mercutio now seems half angry, as he laughingly deals his last blows, a few coarse sexual remarks; then he, too, gives up. They go away, Benvolio commenting that there is no use in looking for someone who does not want to be found. As they leave, Romeo, who has overheard it all and must be thankful for Benvolio's characteristic tact, mutters to himself a retort to Mercutio's derision: "He jests at scars that never felt a wound." This completes the rhyme scheme of the sequence and puts a poignant end to the jocose indecencies.

COMMENT

Romeo is as passionately lovesick as Mercutio teases him for being, but in a new and different way, and with a different woman. The humor and pathos of the scene are caused by the fact that Mercutio is not aware of this new twist, and all his pointed, ribald remarks fly far afield without his knowing it. At the same time, they come dangerously close to hitting home. Throughout the scene we can see Romeo, crouching close to the other side of the fence, listening with mixed emotions to comments that have lost their sting and yet offend his new-found young passion. It is this that elicits his own whispered retort to Mercutio, as if to say "you joke about old, healed scars of love, but you have never even felt a wound such as I now have to suffer."

ACT II, SCENE 2

No sooner have Mercutio's raucous laughter and jokes echoed down the street for the last time, than Romeo sees a window illuminated in Capulet's house and a girlish figure standing there. "But soft! what light through yonder window breaks?/ It is the east, and Juliet is the sun." These words break from him, beginning his famous soliloquy (a speech spoken by one character, to himself or herself alone). The conceits of romantic love return with renewed life and vigor. The moon, he thinks, is sick and pale with jealousy at Juliet's brilliance. As she steps full into view on the balcony, Romeo can at first do little but exclaim "O, it is my love!" and wish to tell her so. He feels that she is speaking, and he wants to answer, but he falls back shyly. Instead he becomes enraptured with her eyes, calling them stars; and her cheeks, which would make real stars dim in comparison; and again her eyes, which, if they were set in heaven, would make birds think it was daylight by their brightness.

COMMENT

This speech, and the entire scene to come, is conventional, almost formal. At the same time, this speech begins a sustained flow of pure lyricism that lasts throughout the scene. Romeo is enthralled. Juliet is the light of day in darkness to him, and his speech moves among images expressing this light: the sun, the moon, the stars. She appears like a revelation of some high truth in the middle of dark chaos. Romeo's speech is even slightly confused, as indeed he is himself, caught between being struck dumb and finding poetry welling out naturally from his mouth.

The scene on the stage would clearly embody Romeo's impassioned imagery. Juliet would be on one of the balconies that were part of the construction of an Elizabethan theater. Standing high above her lover, she would seem to be all that he named her. There would be some distance between Romeo below and Juliet above, and the tension of this distance would be used to enhance and carry along this long ardor that they share.

Juliet, high on her balcony, is so filled with emotion at their recent meeting that all she says is "Ay, me!" She does not know that her lover is in the garden below, and she is lost in remembering. Romeo, delighted to hear her voice, breathes out praises. To him, she is a "bright angel," a messenger from

heaven before whom mortals fall thunderstruck. She lights up the whole sky. But when Juliet speaks again, she is mournful: "O, Romeo, Romeo!" Why must her love be Romeo, a Montague and an enemy? She wishes she could deny her name; and she offers, if he loves her, to give up her own name, presumably by marrying him. For only the name is an enemy, not anything that is an inseparable part of Romeo, the man. She vows that if he will give up his name, he shall have all of her in exchange. Romeo, stepping from the shadows, takes her at her word, declaring aloud that he will be Romeo no longer.

COMMENT

Romeo's continuing comparison of Juliet to divinity, and to all sources of light, is cut off by her spoken thoughts. In speaking her wishes into the night, Juliet has unknowingly declared her love to her lover. She is very innocent and shy; she would not have spoken so openly on purpose. In puzzling over the menace that lies in his name, she has introduced a more somber note to the rhapsody. But the newness and wonder felt by the lovers in this shining religion of love shortly overcome even this.

Hearing Romeo speak up to renounce his name, Juliet is startled and demands to know who has overheard her. But he cannot tell her his name, as he has just given it up for love of her. She knows his voice, however; and when she asks if he is Romeo, a Montague, he replies that he is not, if she dislikes the name. In reality, this giving up the names is a token of love, and the pair know that they cannot renounce what they have been born to. Juliet first fears for Romeo's safety, but he brushes this aside, declaring that no walls or danger could daunt his love. He fears more from one hostile glance of her eyes than from the swords of her relatives. Eased by Romeo's assurances, Juliet softens to shy, gentle coquetry: If it were not for the "mask of night," he would see her blush at having been overheard. "Fain would I dwell on form," she says, and withdraw what was spoken, so that they might pursue a formal courtship. But it is too late for that. In the profusion of her love, she asks first that he swears he loves her, and then, if he thinks she is too quickly won, she promises she will deny her love, so that he may court her. Otherwise, she would never deny it.

COMMENT

The lover's speeches run over into each other, so excited and joyful are they. Juliet, who is so truly untried, is overcome at the strength of her own feeling, and her thoughts bound and rebound between expressing her love and keeping her proper distance, so that Romeo will not love her less for being forward. The themes of formality and convention find direct expression here. Both are a little shy at the speed of things and would like to linger through the courtship, savoring the sweetness of the flirtations and declarations of love. But their situation, an emergency that they cannot ignore, does not allow it. They will proceed most unconventionally, marrying speedily and flouting all parental demands. Their love makes them individuals and rebels, contrasting them with the rest of the conventional world. Still, they court and flirt now, while they can.

Romeo wants only to swear his love, and he swears by the moon. Juliet does not want that, as the moon is not constant, but has its phases. If he must swear he must swear by himself; but when he starts to do so, she again cuts him short. She wants no swearing. Their love has been so beautiful to her that she is afraid it will end as suddenly as it began, like a fateful flash of lightning. Juliet would prefer that the bud of their love have time to blossom. To allow for that, she would say goodnight now, but Romeo detains her. He wants to exchange vows, but Juliet has given hers, and more would just be extra. Still, when she hears her Nurse calling her, she finds she can't bear to leave Romeo, and tells him to wait until she can come back. While she is gone, Romeo speaks to the night: "O blessed night! I am afeared,/ Being in night, all this is but a dream,/ Too flattering-sweet to be substantial."

COMMENT

Both lovers fear the fleeting, momentary quality of their love. Juliet compares the love to a brief flash of lightning in the darkness, a short brilliance in the night. Romeo blesses the night, for it has brought him joy; yet, at the same time, he fears that the joy may be no more than a dream coming during a night's sleep. The lovers love the night, which lets their love shine out, but they sense a menace in it—the same menace of the impermanent and vulnerable as was spoken of by Mercutio as "vain fantasy," in Act I, Scene 4.

Juliet returns to her window. Whispering hastily to her lover while her Nurse calls to her from the room behind, she says that if he wishes to marry her, Romeo should send word the next day by her messenger. If not, she pleads that he leave her alone. Again she vanishes within, while Romeo finds the night impossible without her light. Yet one last time she reappears, just as he is going, and calls him. She wants only to ask what time she should send her messenger tomorrow. She has forgotten her real purpose in calling him back. Perhaps it was just to linger a bit longer with him. The two do not want to say goodnight yet, and Juliet embroiders their lingering with her playfulness: She would like him to go, but no farther than a pet bird on a string who can be tugged back when its mistress wants, "So loving-jealous of its liberty." Only she knows that if he were her bird, she might kill him with too much loving. At last, calling "Good night, good night! parting is such sweet sorrow/ That I shall say good night till it be morrow," Juliet goes in for the last time. Romeo stands a moment in the darkness; then he departs for a visit to his priest and confessor.

COMMENT

Using the ancient device of lovers who do not wish to part from each other, Shakespeare strung out his duet just a bit longer. He finally released the audience gently back to earth with Romeo's last words.

ACT II, SCENE 3

It is early morning, and Friar Laurence, the monk who is Romeo's confessor, is up and about already. He is educated in the lore of herbs and their powers; and since herbs, if they are to keep their full potency, must be gathered before the sun has dried the dew from their leaves, he goes out at dawn to fill his "osier cage," or basket, "With baleful weeds and precious-juiced flowers./ The earth that's nature's mother is her tomb;/ What is her burying grave, that is her womb." The good Friar comments on the cycle of life, on plants growing from the earth and decaying back into it. All things in nature, even the most vile, have a special function and good use on earth. At the same time, the Friar knows that even the best things on earth can be misused for the purpose of evil. Both properties can exist in the same plant; for example, an herb can be beneficial to the health if smelled, but poisonous if eaten. Everything lies in how we use what nature gives us, and this is true even of human beings, who can use or misuse their own inherent qualities, so causing themselves to be good or evil.

COMMENT

After the necessary yet deliriously lyrical interlude during which Romeo and Juliet have established their special love, we return to the demands of the action. Although the previous scene seems swift when we remember that in it an entire courtship took place, it had the nature of a beautiful pause. The pace now must pick up. Friar Laurence's long speech begins with a description of grey dawn coming with smiles to chase away night, and with it comes the time when the day's work must be resumed. The speech allows for the modulation from night to day, from ease to activity.

The Friar's speech shows him to be a good soul, with a philosophical turn of mind. He is aware of the powers of his knowledge of herbs, and his intention always will be to use these powers for the furthering of good, not evil. This well-intentioned quality in the Friar, coupled with his knowledge of drugs, plays an important part in the development of the plot, when the lovers find it necessary to try and extricate themselves from dangerous complications.

Romeo, who has been up all night wooing Juliet, now comes to see the Friar. The Friar is surprised to see him, feeling that a youth, with no cares to make him sleepless, should still be sleeping at this hour, or else must be disturbed in mind or body. He feels this is not so in Romeo's case, and guesses that he had not been to bed at all. Romeo acknowledges the truth of the guess, while quickly assuring the Friar that "the sweeter rest" he had was not with Rosaline, for he has forgotten her and the sadness she brought him. Romeo riddles the Friar a bit, saying he has been with his enemy, who has wounded him and been wounded by him, but that the cure for both their wounds is within the monk's "holy physic," or sacred healing power. He quickly clarifies things, however, telling the Friar that he and Juliet have pledged their love for each other, and that it only remains for the Friar to join them forever in marriage that very day.

COMMENT

Romeo not only respects the Friar but shares a camaraderie with him, as is made evident by the Friar's pleased questioning about why Romeo is not asleep—and by Romeo's light-hearted punning about the wounds of love and their remedy, marriage. This love of Romeo for Juliet has not left him mournful, as he was over Rosaline, but full of high-spirited joy, even in the face of serious obstacles. Nothing can be quick enough for him; he loves without restraint, and with all the impetuosity of the young, and he must make their love sanctified and eternal by immediate marriage.

Friar Laurence, bowled over by this abrupt change, comments on the changefulness of youth. Only yesterday Romeo cried salt tears for a love that did not even last long enough to be seasoned by that salt. The Friar's ears still ring with Romeo's groans; and while he had encouraged Romeo to bury that love, he didn't intend that another love should spring up instantly. Still, he admits that he felt that Romeo was loving according to a book he could scarcely even read yet. Apparently, the Friar senses from Romeo's elation that this is not love by the book, but the real thing. Also, he hopes that the love and marriage of a Montague to a Capulet might force an alliance between the two feuding houses, changing the hate between them to love. On hearing this approval, Romeo cries, "O, let us hence; I stand on sudden haste." To this impetuousness the monk replies, "Wisely and slow; they stumble that run fast."

COMMENT

For all his forbearance, the Friar is here contrasted with Romeo. Although he ends by approving the marriage, he cautions Romeo against hurting himself by being hasty. The Friar is sympathetic, but even he cannot understand the urgency that is inherent in this love. He remains rational and wise. He wishes Romeo would be, too, because he does not grasp that the very nature of the feeling rules out all caution and rationality. Romeo and Juliet have a sympathizer, but their love remains beyond his understanding. Because of the chasm between their emotions and all rationality, they stand essentially alone.

SUMMARY

The following have been treated in this scene:

(1) Herbs and potions, which can do both good and evil, depending on how they are used.

(2) The possibility of the love between Romeo and Juliet serving to bridge the gap between their families.

(3) The irrevocable, involuntary, and irrational speed of Romeo and Juliet's romantic fervor leads them to immediate action, without reflection, and accounts for the amazing velocity of the play. This love is on a pinnacle, beyond the understanding of those not moved by it. It promises not only to be speedy, but to be very much alone, shared only by the lovers. Even the kindly Friar cannot keep the two lovers company in their flight of love.

ACT II, SCENE 4

Mercutio and Benvolio, abroad in Verona this morning, wonder where Romeo is. They know that he has not been home, and they fear that Rosaline will drive him mad. Tybalt, angered by Romeo's uninvited appearance at the Capulet festival, has sent him a challenge to duel. Benvolio feels sure that Romeo will answer not just the letter, but the man and the dare; but Mercutio says that Romeo is already dead—slain by a woman's eye, a love song, and Cupid's arrow—and not prepared to fight Tybalt. "Why, what is Tybalt?" asks Benvolio. In lore, Tybalt is the name for the prince of cats. Mercutio punningly states that this Tybalt is more than prince of cats; he is a master of the laws of ceremony, one who fights with a sense of timing as natural to him as keeping time to music is to those who sing. Yet Mercutio clearly despises Tybalt, despite his skill with a sword, and goes on to make fun of him as a silly dandy who is at least as concerned with having fashionable manners and clothes as he is with fighting like a true gentleman.

COMMENT

Mercutio's witty sally on Tybalt makes clear to us that he detests the man, finding him despicable, shallow, ridiculous, and lacking in true manliness. But it also makes a point of Tybalt's being an adept fighter, no small adversary to Romeo. Tybalt's challenge to Romeo is indeed serious, as we find out later. Mercutio's extreme dislike of Tybalt is equally serious and important.

Just now, Romeo comes into view, and the two men begin a chanting tease. Mercutio calls him a dried herring, without its roe. He means that without Rosaline, Romeo is like a herring without its mate: He dries up and becomes "fishified." Running through various heroines of literature, Mercutio states the faults Romeo must find in them in comparison with Rosaline. But he is glad to see Romeo, and he ribs his friend about having slipped away the previous evening. Romeo, just come from the Friar, is in a fine, delighted frame of mind; he warms up to the fast-flying witticisms immediately. He scores many good returns over Mercutio as their conversation skips about. Periodically Mercutio, delighted at Romeo's return to free-spirited word play, protests that Romeo is in excellent form: "Thy wit is very bitter sweeting; it is a most sharp sauce." Romeo retorts that Mercutio is a "broad goose," using "broad" to mean obvious, indecent, and unrestrained all at once. Mercutio, pleased beyond answering, bursts out: "Now art thou sociable, now art thou Romeo; now art thou what thou art, by art as well as by nature," and adds the sexual pun that love had made Romeo "hide his bauble (the stick carried by a fool or jester) in a hole." Benvolio stops Mercutio there, to prevent his tale from becoming "large" (meaning both long and licentious).

COMMENT

This scene has been like a fast set of tennis, the verbal ball bouncing merrily back and forth. Romeo is truly in love. Gone are his attitudes of despondency. He is joyful, and his spirited sense of humor has returned full force, allowing him to exceed even his old self in light-hearted repartee. Mercutio, who loves him, is overjoyed not only at Romeo's clever words but at his return to his full self. In saying "Now art thou what thou art, by art as well as by nature," Mercutio is not only playing happily with words. He has stated his basic belief: A man must be himself, no matter what; he must be true to his own nature and strengthen it by the use of his mind. He must be self-sufficient, must stand alone on the hard ground of reality, without the romance of such ideals as love or dreams. And yet, as we shall see with respect to Mercutio, a man must stand for and respond to what he believes and feels. These few short words to Romeo are the key to Mercutio's life and death.

As the friends conclude their jest, the Nurse and her servant Peter arrive. The Nurse is the messenger Juliet promised to send to Romeo. She is on an errand of courtship and is about to speak with aristocrats. It is a role she enjoys; and to play it to the full, she affects the airs of a lady of breeding, holding a fan before her face in modesty as she approaches. After one quip to the effect that her fan is prettier than her face, Mercutio falls in with the play-acting and greets her as a gentlewoman, only to instantly affront her assumed gentility by saying, "The bawdy hand of the dial is now upon the prick of noon." Romeo, and even gentle Benvolio, fall in with this spirit of raillery for and at the Nurse. Mercutio even breaks into song, intimating that the Nurse is a prostitute now gone stale with age. He and Benvolio depart, leaving Romeo to share the confidence the Nurse has requested.

COMMENT

The Nurse reveals herself beautifully in her attempt at discreet, ladylike demeanor with the young bachelors. She is conscious of and enjoys her own affectation. She is not really offended at their making fun of her; she enjoys that and the bawdy jokes without ever letting her airs drop. For all his lightness, Romeo must know immediately that she comes from Juliet, and he thus must be eager to talk with her.

Referring to Mercutio, the Nurse asks who that rogue was. True to the role she has chosen, her sense of dignity is offended by him. She must express this to Romeo, and in the vigor with which she does so she lets her demure facade drop: "Scurvy knave! I am none of his flirt-gills" (that is, not one of Mercutio's loose, flirtatious wenches). Resuming the role, she chides Peter for not defending her; then she turns to Romeo and gets down to business. First, she warns Romeo that he had better not be playing double with her young mistress. Romeo protests, telling the Nurse of his hopes to marry Juliet that very afternoon in Friar Laurence's cell. He urges that Juliet find a means to be there. He also promises to send a ladder, which shall be his means for reaching Juliet tonight so that they may consummate their marriage. All this the Nurse promises to relay to her mistress. True to herself, she must prattle away a bit about Paris, his suit for Juliet's hand, and how Juliet turns pale when the Nurse teasingly says that Paris is the more handsome. She tells him that Juliet has some small verse about Romeo and rosemary. (Rosemary is the flower of remembrance, used at weddings and—ironically in this case—at funerals.) Romeo breaks this off, and leaves.

COMMENT

This is the Nurse's scene. She is herself in the role of lady she has chosen to play, and equally herself in her lapses from that role. We feel concerned that her meandering memory will fail to transmit Romeo's messages correctly. At the same time, we are amused at her changes of attitude and at her description of "sometimes" teasing Juliet, as if the love affair between her mistress and Romeo had been going on for some weeks now, instead of a bare twelve hours. In the minds of both the lovers and the audience the love is at once as young as twelve hours and as ancient as all love. In the midst of her chattering, the Nurse's reference to the proposed marriage of Juliet to Paris, which will have its effect on the line of action, strikes an ominous undertone, as does her mention of the rosemary. We also may notice here that there is no indication of Romeo's feeling jealous at the mention of Paris. The lovers have clasped hands, a sign of giving trust, and neither one ever doubts the other.

SUMMARY

Much has happened in this scene.

(1) Romeo has blossomed, and shown his full self, in the witticisms that spring from his inner happiness. His old attitudes are gone forever, and we see that the value of his stereotyped love for Rosaline is to contrast with, and so help define, this new, completely untypical, individual love.

(2) Mercutio, Romeo's closest companion, has been presented still more clearly and has voiced his keynote of being true to oneself. His jolly sensuality and his realism are contrasted with and used to help define Romeo, who endorses the idealisms of love and dreams, and whose wit emerges from these rather than from realism.

(3) The Nurse, Juliet's closest companion, is to Juliet what Mercutio is to Romeo—a balancing, contrasting force of the more realistic and baser instincts of life. She, like Mercutio, is true to herself, even when she plays a role. The sensuality of both these companions to the hero and heroine is always out in the open, never obscene.

(4) The arrangements for the immediate marriage and the wedding night have been made. This forwards the plot and

the progress of the love affair. Everything is moving swiftly now. This scene, which is a long one, has gone rapidly. Beneath the impetuous speed we are reminded of the ever-present threats to the lovers' happiness.

ACT II, SCENE 5

Alone in her father's orchard, Juliet waits impatiently for her Nurse to return with Romeo's message. The Nurse promised she would be back in half an hour, but for three long hours Juliet has waited. It is now noon, and the young girl is in a small frenzy. She wishes her messengers to Romeo could be thoughts, which would fly like doves or the wings of the wind, driving back the shadows of the hills as they fly. It seems a long journey that the sun has traveled from morning to midday. If the Nurse were as young and full of passion as Juliet, she would move between the two lovers like a tossed ball, carrying their messages. Though Juliet knows the Nurse is old and slow, this much delay seems to her to result from someone pretending to be dead.

COMMENT

Juliet's impatience as she waits to hear if she is to be married equals Romeo's. She loves and thinks of him with all the powers of her imagination, and her reckless, loving thoughts rival Romeo's for their beauty of imagery. No speed is enough for her, she is so caught in the flood of their love. She cannot feel complete unless the passion they share is advancing full speed ahead.

The Nurse and Peter now come, and Juliet greets the Nurse with high excitement. Peter is sent out, and she questions the Nurse urgently. But the Nurse, as if in answer to Juliet's previous remark on old people, only complains about her weary joints. Juliet has no sympathy at present; she wishes the Nurse had her young bones and that she had the Nurse's news. The Nurse only retorts that her mistress can wait till she has caught her breath. Juliet is getting irritated; the Nurse has spent more breath complaining than the answer to the question "Is thy news good or bad?" would take. In answer, the Nurse takes a tone of derision and uses it to praise highly Juliet's choice of a husband. Juliet knows Romeo's value; all she wants to hear is whether or not they will be married. Again the Nurse returns to patter about her aches and pains. Driven to distraction, Juliet has been unsympathetic to the ailments of old age; so the Nurse, partly out of perversity and partly from desire to be pitied and given attention, will play this game until her young mistress shows some response to her complaints. Seeing this at last, and regretting her own unresponsiveness, Juliet softens, caressing her Nurse. But when the Nurse teasingly starts to relinquish her news, only to interrupt herself with a question about the whereabouts of Lady Capulet, it is the last straw. Juliet speaks crossly and abruptly, with real irritation. Only then does the Nurse answer, in a short, concise, and surprisingly accurate speech, describing the plans for the marriage this afternoon at the Friar's and for the ladder that will let Romeo come to his bride and consummate their marriage that evening. Juliet joyfully departs for Friar Laurence's cell.

COMMENT

The Nurse pettishly teases Juliet now, even as we have seen Mercutio taunt Romeo. She wants her share of attention and thanks. Her concern over her own physical condition—partly real and partly pretended—suggests her natural, defensible egotism. Juliet shows a slight degree of the same quality in her single-minded efforts to extract the news, but she has passion on her side. The Nurse is actually being quite cruel. Yet when she relents and tells her news, she does so with a genuine acknowledgment of how Juliet must be feeling. She gently chides her mistress's blushes, and she calls Romeo's coming by ladder at night his ascent to "a bird's nest." The delays before the telling dramatically contrast with the previous and coming scenes, and thus make the audience share the urgency of Juliet's emotion. The device also enhances the contrast between the slow, unemotional state of age and the blinding speed of youth in love. Notice that Romeo, the Nurse, Juliet, and even the Friar think of the marriage and its consummation as being one, a whole in which both parts are equally holy.

ACT II, SCENE 6

It is the time and place of the wedding. Romeo and Friar Laurence speak quietly to each other as they wait for Juliet. The Friar asks for heaven's smile on the marriage, so that it may not be followed by sorrow. Romeo adds his "Amen"; for him, however, no amount of sorrow can weigh more strongly than the joy of a moment with his bride. If the Friar only joins their hands in holy marriage, he will dare "love-devouring death" to do whatever it might. He will have named her for his own, and that is enough. The Friar answers with characteristic moderation and wisdom: "These violent delights have violent ends,/ And in their triumph die, like fire and powder,/ Which as they kiss consume." He enjoins Romeo to love moderately, so that he may love long.

COMMENT

Romantic love of this total, all-embracing, rapid kind has full sway over both lovers. They accept it, revel in it, and by doing so unwittingly taunt death. The Friar's words are a true prophecy. The kind of love that these two have chosen and surrendered to cannot, by its very nature, be moderate or long-lasting. We cannot picture Romeo and Juliet continuing through the normal cycle of prospering and waning love, of children, of middle and old age. They have only their being now, as intense lovers. Their love can do only that against which the Friar warns: meet, light up in a brief, brilliant flame, consume itself, and end in an unlooked-for death. This is what will happen, and it is what Romeo and Juliet have chosen without realizing.

The Friar's moderation would be impossible for them, and they do not want it. They have staked a claim on the highest form of love, where the spiritual and the earthly unite. Others cannot understand this, and the lovers are alone.

As Juliet comes, her step is so light that Romeo fancies it would not break the gossamer of summer air. She greets the "ghostly" (spiritual) Friar. The imaginations of both Romeo and Juliet are on fire. If her joy leaps up as high as his, Romeo bids her to sweeten the air with the music of her imaginings about the love they will share. Her answer is that she must speak of substance, not ornament, but that the substance of her love is so great that she cannot add up half the wealth of it. The Friar then takes them to his inner chamber, where he will by "Holy church incorporate two in one."

COMMENT

This is the wedding, where Romeo and Juliet will "die" as two separate individuals in order to become joined and unified. Their love for each other is not voiced in terms of the sensual or corporeal; rather, it is expressed as the delight of freed imaginations and of more feeling than can be expressed. Their speeches form a short but highly charged antiphony as they go to their union.

SUMMARY

The whole act, which began with the courtship in the orchard, has progressed quickly but with changing pace, to this quiet climax in marriage. For the audience, the true fatal nature of the love becomes more vivid as the lovers are united forever. The threat of the feud, and the ominous prophecy of the Friar, have subtly built up the sense of underlying danger and prepared us for the act to come. This wedding ceremony is a calm before a storm.

ROMEO AND JULIET
ACT III

ACT III, SCENE 1

The afternoon has drawn on after the wedding and has become hot. Benvolio, who is with Mercutio, observes that hot weather makes hot tempers; and since the Capulets are about, he pleads that they go home and escape more fighting. Mercutio, who feels mischievous, jestingly accuses Benvolio of really wanting a fight, and of being quick to pick one over slight excuses, such as a man cracking nuts when Benvolio has hazel eyes. Benvolio maintains that if he were as soon moved to quarrel as is Mercutio, his life would not be worth a "fee-simple." At this juncture the Capulets do appear, Tybalt in the lead. Mercutio cares not; and at Tybalt's request for a word with them, he tauntingly suggests that he ask for a word and a blow. He dares Tybalt to find a reason for fighting him. He pretends that Tybalt has called himself and Benvolio "minstrels," a faintly derogatory word implying vagabonds, and he draws his sword as a fiddler draws his bow, to make Tybalt dance. He is deliberately provoking the antagonistic Capulet. When Benvolio suggests that the two of them should either keep their quarrel rational or go some place private, Mercutio refuses to budge.

COMMENT

The contrast with the preceding scene is vivid. Mercutio, his high spirits subjected to the sluggish heat, is in fact feeling quarrelsome. From his speech earlier this morning, we know that he has profound distaste for Tybalt. He disregards peace-loving Benvolio's pleas, and he tries to antagonize this man whom he so dislikes.

Romeo, married only an hour earlier, appears just at the crucial point. Despite Mercutio's jabs, it is Romeo that Tybalt wants to fight: "Here come my man." But Mercutio is angered at Tybalt's resistance to his gibes, and he takes this remark of

Tybalt's in its lowest sense, that of calling Romeo a servant. Tybalt deliberately insults Romeo, trying to entice him to a duel. But Romeo's state of mind has transcended the sarcastic irony of such name-calling as "The love I bear thee can afford/ No better term than this—thou art a villain." No one knows of the marriage but Romeo and the audience; as a result, Romeo's suspenseful pause, and the riddling response he gives, is perplexing to everyone on the stage. Tybalt refuses to be forgiven for slandering; he has no intention of missing his chance to revenge the grudge he holds. But Romeo continues his mysterious talk of loving the Capulet name as well as his own. His comrades are astonished.

COMMENT

We must examine Romeo's responses. Perhaps he is so uplifted by being now one with Juliet that he views this petty picking of fights from a supreme distance and can react only with all-embracing love to the insults of his new cousin. Perhaps his immediate reaction is to seek vengeance, but he has effectively squelched the impulse and holds it under control in the light of his new relationship to Tybalt. Tybalt has seen Romeo intruding at a family party and perhaps has observed Romeo's attention to Juliet, which would only add insult to injury. To Benvolio and Mercutio, Romeo must still appear as Rosaline's lovesick pup, too weak to put his manhood to the test of a duel. And to Mercutio, such weakening love bears all the marks of self-indulgent idealism. This action of Romeo's infuriates him, even though the feud is not his.

Mercutio, livid, cries out, "O calm, dishonorable, vile submission!" and draws on Tybalt, saying that he means to have one of the nine lives of the king of cats. Tybalt answers by drawing and, ignoring Romeo's cry to Mercutio to stop, they fight. Romeo then draws himself, calling to Benvolio to help him, and rushes to break up the fight. As he tries to separate his cousin and his friend, he blocks one of Mercutio's parries. As Tybalt and his followers withdraw, Mercutio clutches his side, saying, "I am hurt,/ A plague o' both your houses. I am sped," a cry which he repeats more than once while the scene lasts. At Mercutio's "Ay, ay, a scratch, a scratch; marry, 'tis enough," Romeo is stricken. To his inquiries Mercutio replies that the cut is "not so deep as a well, nor so wide as a church door," but that it is enough to make him a "grave" man by tomorrow. An abusive torrent bursts from Mercutio, who vilifies Tybalt as "a dog, a rat, a mouse, a cat, to scratch a man to death! a braggart, a rogue, a villian, that fights by the book of arithmetic!" Why did Romeo try to come between them? It was this, says Mercutio, that caused the fatal wound. Romeo did what he thought would be best, but Mercutio again curses both houses, and turns to Benvolio to be carried out. Romeo stands stunned, muttering painfully to himself at the indignity he feels over what has happened, and confirming Mercutio's thoughts in a simpler and stronger speech than he has yet used: "O sweet Juliet,/ Thy beauty hath made me effeminate,/ And in my temper soften'd valour's steel." Almost immediately Benvolio returns. Mercutio, the "gallant spirit" that scorned the earth, is dead. Romeo can see nothing but the darkness of this day, and many more to come. He bows his head to this new fate.

COMMENT

This scene, long prepared for by the hovering feud, by the presentation of Mercutio's vibrant character, and by our understanding of Tybalt as well, now marks the turning of the play from high romance to tragedy. Mercutio, whose creed is to be true to himself, could not but be enraged and deeply offended by what seems to him the lily-livered conduct of the friend he loves. If Romeo lacks the pride in himself necessary to retaliate to Tybalt's despicable taunts, Mercutio will do it. To him, Tybalt is a low animal that crawls on his belly, lives by a lifeless set of rules, and scratches its prey to death. The realistic, ironic, life-loving Mercutio finds that his only choice is to defend manhood and selfhood against such infamies, and so, despite himself, he dies for an ideal. Dying, he does not give up his fight, but puns wryly and cynically, and curses violently, until he has no more breath. The lyricism of Queen Mab has guttered out with a growl. The audience has heard much of Mercutio, and we feel his was a precious spirit.

Suddenly, furious Tybalt shows himself again. This is too much for Romeo. Abruptly he casts away the "respective lenity" that had resulted from his marriage. He calls to Tybalt that Mercutio's soul is waiting, and one or both of theirs must accompany it. Tybalt's answer rings: it will have to be Romeo's soul. The two fall to furious, earnest fencing, and Romeo kills his new cousin. As Tybalt falls, Mercutio is avenged, and Romeo has at last stood for his own honor. Benvolio cries to him, "Away, away," for the citizens are aroused and the newly established penalty for such fighting is death. Romeo groans, "O, I am fortune's fool!" and forces himself to run off.

COMMENT

Romeo has been hurled from his position of ecstasy to one of pitiful misery, and in this turnabout he shows himself to be of stern fiber. Without the smallest indulgence in superfluous grief, he has trumpeted out his challenge to Tybalt. The loss of Mercutio must be repaid in kind. On having killed the man, Romeo is yet more deeply stunned. With his fate a ringing menace in his ears, he gathers his strength, accepts his fate, and leaves. Northrop Frye applies the Elizabethans' high regard for male friendships to this scene, concluding that Shakespeare is overturning convention by showing that when "male friendship overrides love of women, . . . Romeo becomes irrevocably a tragic figure."

Citizens come running; close on their heels come both the

feuding households and Verona's Prince. Amidst cries for vengeance, Benvolio explains to Prince Escalus what has occurred. He perhaps exaggerates Romeo's humility, and in the exaggeration lie tones not only of his desire to protect Romeo but also of his annoyance at Romeo's conduct. The tale is otherwise vivid and true to the facts. Lady Capulet accuses him of natural prejudice in favor of the Montagues, and asks for Romeo's death. Lord Montague's answer is that Romeo only gave Tybalt the punishment coming to him. The Prince ponders, weighing both sides. His conclusion is that Romeo shall be exiled, and that for the pointless loss of Mercutio, one of his own family, he shall exact heavy fines from both the feuding households. Romeo must leave Verona immediately. If he is caught first, he will be put to death. The Prince can have no more mercy, for his past leniency has seemed only to give license to more murdering.

COMMENT

Here, in the very core of the play, justice is once more meted out by the Prince. His first appearance was at the play's beginning, when the fatal feud revived. He comes now at the play's turning, when the chain of what seem to be accidents has culminated in loss. The peace he requested has resulted in the grievous death of one of his own relatives. He serves here as a figure of justice and of a sterner, more forcefully demanded peace. His presence ends the chaos and the loss that have ensued since the scene began. Some order is restored. But imposed on the lovers is a fate of what would seem to be eternal separation. That is the punishment hardest to bear, and the justice that seems least just. The Prince, who marks always the structural points in the plot when fate and chance clash with cataclysmic effect, will come again only at the play's end.

SUMMARY

The gathering speed and ill-omen of the play have found a

climax in the tragic loss of Mercutio, a character we treasured, and in the exile of Romeo from Verona. Accident has again reared its head as a determinant of action, and we now realize that it is fate.

(1) The death of Mercutio proves to be the play's turning point. From here the love of Romeo and Juliet will hurtle them down to doom.

(2) Youth and Romeo, which stand for love, have again clashed against the hate of the elders who initiated this feud; in doing so they only have furthered the cause of hate and war, while trying to do the opposite.

(3) Romeo has again broadened and deepened in character; first by refusing to fight with his new cousin Tybalt; next, by accepting the burden of vengeance for his friend Mercutio, recognizing it as his honor and duty, and killing Tybalt, despite his relationship; and finally by accepting the fate that all this has brought upon him.

ACT III, SCENE 2

Juliet, unaware of what has just happened, waits out the passing of the day in her father's orchard. She is more impatient than ever, for tonight Romeo is to come to her as her husband. At the opening of the scene, she delivers an impassioned soliloquy, well known as "Juliet's invocation to the night." Beginning with "Gallop apace, you fiery-footed steeds," she urges the sun on to its setting in the west, so that night may arrive sooner. "Spread thy close curtains, love-performing night." She longs for the shelter of darkness, when Romeo can come to her unseen. The dark suits lovers, for love is blind and the beauty of lovers is enough light for them. Juliet compares night to a "sober-suited matron, all in black," who will teach her how to lose the game of love to her lover. Only by losing can she win. Changing the image to one of falconry, this tender girl compares herself to a falcon, a bird of prey used by hunters for catching pheasants and quail. Until released for the kill, a falcon is kept quiet by having its head enclosed in a small black hood. When nervous or anxious for the kill, a falcon will "bate," or beat its wings rapidly. So Juliet hopes that night will "Hood my unmann'd blood, bating in my cheeks." With the word "unmann'd" she had used the language of falconry to refer to her own virginity. She invokes night, and she invokes Romeo, the lover who is "day in night," and who will glide on the wings of night like "new snow on a raven's back." All she asks is that this night bring Romeo to her. After that, if he dies (which Juliet does not imagine) the night may take him back, may set him in the heaven with stars. Then "All the world will be in love with night, And pay no worship to the garish sun." For love belongs to Juliet now that she is married, but she does not own it, and she can't own love until Romeo possesses her. Because of that she is waiting now, as impatiently as a child waits for a festival.

COMMENT

The soliloquy is a magnificent one. From the vigor of its opening lines, on through all the changes of tone and pace, the speech shows Juliet in a new light. Her voice has more resonance, her images more strength, and her passionate imagination more maturity. Despite the fact that there is a profusion of images, all coming hard and fast, the soliloquy is based on the unifying images of night and light. Juliet courts this night, which by its darkness will allow Romeo's safe journey to her and will teach her how to perform the act of love, how to play the game she must lose in order to win. The only light she needs is Romeo himself, who is "day in night." The light of day and the "garish sun" offer nothing to her; they are only "tedious." It is night that is "loving," for it blesses her love with its darkness and silence, and lets that love shine out. Even the stars, emblems of the fate she does not recognize, seem to be good: Romeo will be made eternal by the stars. And here, remembering what has happened in the preceding scene, we are struck by the tragic irony of Juliet's whole rapturous speech: It is like singing in the face of death. So does Juliet hasten the coming of her wedding night.

Now the Nurse comes, carrying with her the very cords Romeo has prepared to let him come to his wife tonight. They are to be thrown over the balcony so that he may climb up. To Juliet these ropes, as well as any word connected with Romeo, are harbingers of joy. But the Nurse flings the ropes to the ground and with shocking sorrow, begins to mourn: "He's gone, he's killed, he's dead." Juliet, assuming the Nurse means Romeo, can only say, "Can heaven be so envious?" By envious she means not only jealous of their happiness, but malicious. The Nurse takes the latter meaning and retorts that Romeo can be envious. This is more than Juliet can bear, and she bursts out, "What devil art thou that dost torment me thus? This torture should be roar'd in dismal hell." She demands to know if Romeo has killed himself; and playing on the various meanings of "I," "aye," and "eye," she makes it clear that her misery hangs on the Nurse's answer. The Nurse, who is never straightforward enough to give a simple answer, does not answer yes or no; instead, she launches into a gory description of how she saw the wound with her own eyes. Juliet, beside herself with dismay, cries, "O break, my heart!" and "Vile earth, to earth resign, end motion here." The only interpretation that she can give to the Nurse's words is that Romeo is dead—and that is Juliet's own death sentence.

COMMENT

The sudden news of tragedy has abruptly descended on Juliet, and the reversal of her fortunes changes her rapture to misery. She does not know the truth of what has happened, but suspecting the worst, she is swallowed up by grief. The Nurse, who is always one to relish any occasion where her own sentimentality can be indulged, has gone about delivering the news to her young mistress with complete disregard for the girl's feelings. This unnecessary cruelty on the Nurse's part prompts Juliet's anger, and it is an anger with which we sympathize. Age, which is represented by the feuding families, and the lack of true feeling, can afford to dawdle and play meanly with the impetuous emotions of youth. Not only is the Nurse shown in her true self-centered character, grabbing at any chance to indulge her emotions to the fullest, but the elderly woman must squeeze whatever feeling she can from the present tragedy, while young Juliet's feelings run riot before she even knows exactly what has happened.

At last, the Nurse begins to clarify her news. She reveals that it is Tybalt for whom she mourns. Juliet, convinced of Romeo's death, now thinks that both are dead: "Then, dreadful trumpets, sound the general doom!/ For who is living if these two are gone?" But the Nurse finally lets the full blow fall, revealing that Tybalt was killed by Romeo and that Romeo himself is banished. Juliet, by now utterly confused by one reversal after another and worked up to an extreme emotional pitch by the Nurse's playful devices, lets loose a torrent of words that revile the Romeo she loves: "O serpent heart, hid with a flowering face!" and "Despised substance of divinest show!" Using all the opposites of evil and good at her command, she curses her lover as a fiend who hides evil in sweet and even holy trappings. The Nurse picks up this cry; claiming that all this sorrow is making her old, she says, "Shame come to Romeo!" But hearing her curses in the mouth of another brings Juliet to her senses. She retorts with all her spirit, "Blister'd be thy tongue/ For such a wish! he was not born to shame:/ Upon his brow shame is ashamed to sit." Realizing what she herself has just done, Juliet adds, "O, what a beast was I to chide at him."

COMMENT

The Nurse has played on Juliet's emotions and has so

milked the girl's feelings that she is no longer herself. When she finally understands the truth, her fury at Romeo is expressed in conceits and contraries such as we have heard Romeo use about Rosaline. But here the confusion and excess of Juliet's emotional state give the opposites true meaning. We have come full circle, to the point where expressive feeling can find no other means of expression. But the jolt of hearing the Nurse add her imprecation makes Juliet realize what she has said. She turns from cursing her lover to cursing her Nurse; and the dignity with which she declares that Romeo was not born for shame convinces us that this is the true Juliet.

When the Nurse asks Juliet how she can praise the one who killed her cousin, Juliet retorts that she cannot speak badly of her own husband, and is overcome with remorse that she, a newly wedded wife, could mangle her own husband's name. She realizes that had Romeo not killed Tybalt, Tybalt would surely have killed him. She should shed tears of joy that her husband still lives, not tears of sadness at her cousin's death. But she still finds herself crying uncontrollably, no matter what comfort she tries to offer herself. Why? Gradually she begins to remember the word she would rather forget, a word that was worse than news of Tybalt's death: "Banished!" If Tybalt's death wants another grief to keep it company, Juliet would rather it were anything than this. To her, the news of Romeo's exile is worse than news that everyone, including herself, is dead. "There is no end, no limit, measure, bound, In that word's death." The Nurse tells Juliet that her parents are mourning Tybalt, but the girl's tears are all for her lover's banishment. Seeing the cords that Romeo had sent as a "highway" to her bed, and with which the Nurse began this long telling of sad news, Juliet picks them up. She will take them to her wedding bed, "And death, not Romeo, take my maidenhead!" The Nurse finally sees what true depth of misery she has caused Juliet. She is remorseful; and, worrying that her mistress really might kill herself, she offers what comfort she can. She will go find Romeo, who is hiding in the Friar's cell, and make sure that he will come tonight. Juliet brightens at this and hands the Nurse a ring to give to Romeo; it will be a sign that she remains true to him and wants him to come to her.

COMMENT

"Banished" has echoed and re-echoed through these speeches like a refrain of doom. Juliet has recovered herself, only to discover the heaviest grief of all. The cords, which should have been a reminder that tonight the two lovers would joyfully seal their marriage, have instead become a symbol of grief, of marriage not consummated, and even of threatening death. By these artistic devices, Shakespeare impresses upon us the great misery of Juliet. Even the Nurse emerges from her self-involvement and weary old age enough to realize what a cruel blow has been dealt to her mistress in the very heat and anticipation of the coming fulfillment of young love. The last note struck before the scene ends is one of hope in the middle of despair, of a light in the midst of gathering darkness.

SUMMARY

The scene has moved from the gathering brilliance and joy of Juliet's invocation and anticipation of her wedding night to the gathering gloom of tragic banishment and threatened death. Fate seems to be closing in, even while the night, so greatly desired by the lovers, descends. Everything that promised joy now seems an evil omen (even the cords by which Romeo will ascend to his wife's window), and because of this Juliet's speech in opposites is not out of place. The cruelty of the Nurse, who by slowly relishing the moments of grief has driven Juliet to distraction, emphasizes again the separation of the lovers in their youth and swift passion, from the world of old age, rationality, and cruelty. In this scene Juliet—like Romeo in the previous scene—has realized fully what a threat there is to their love and even has participated in it by allowing herself to be tricked into cursing her own husband. She has accepted this threat offered by the rest of the world and at the same time has given herself over completely to her love, sending her ring to Romeo as a token.

ACT III, SCENE 3

Romeo, fearful because he has killed Tybalt, has fled to the safety of Friar Laurence's cell. The Friar, coming from a quick stroll around Verona where he has found news of Romeo's punishment, calls Romeo out from the inner room where he is hiding. When the Friar speaks of Romeo as "wedded to calamity," Romeo asks him what doom the Prince has pronounced. Confident that his news will be of some comfort, the Friar tells Romeo that he is not sentenced to death, but is instead banished from Verona. At this, Romeo cries out abruptly "Ha, banishment! be merciful, say 'death.'" To him, as to Juliet, banishment is worse than death. The world beyond Verona seems to offer nothing but hell, and to be exiled to hell is surely not less than being dead. To say that banishment is less than death is, for Romeo, as cruel as smiling while delivering the death sentence. But to the Friar's way of thinking, Romeo is being rudely unthankful in refusing to see the mercy with which the Prince has ignored the rule that death shall be the punishment for killing.

COMMENT

The similarity between the reactions of Romeo and Juliet to the sentence of exile is very clear. Both lovers consider banishment no better than death. The similarity between this scene and the previous one will become more and more evident. The two scenes balance each other at the center of the play. Contrasted, however, are the two confidants of the lovers: the Friar and the Nurse. Instead of prolonging and falsifying the telling of bad news, the Friar speaks directly, and optimistically, delivering his news in one sentence.

Romeo is not to be so quickly dissuaded from his grief. He has said that any place but Verona is hell. He feels this, just as he feels that wherever Juliet strays is heaven. Dogs, cats, mice, even the flies that feed on decaying flesh will have the honor and "courtship" (that is, the chance at courtliness and the courting) of gazing at Juliet's hands and at her blushing virgin lips. But he, Romeo is banished. He would rather be killed by poison or knives, for the very word kills him. "Banished" is a word for the damned who howl in hell. Romeo wonders how his spiritual confessor, the Friar, can have the heart to use it. The Friar does not want to use the word; he wants to give Romeo the armor to ward off the stings of banishment— namely, philosophy. "Hang up philosophy," says Romeo, unless it can reverse these misfortunes. The Friar wants to discuss Romeo's state philosophically, but Romeo stops him: "Thou cans't not speak of that thou dost not feel." If the Friar were young and in love, if he just had married, if he just had killed a man and been banished, then Romeo feels the Friar might have a right to talk. But, Romeo also feels sure the Friar would not talk; instead he would tear his hair and fall to the ground. So saying, Romeo does throw himself to the ground in a frenzy of despair, "Taking the measure of an unmade grave."

COMMENT

In its wildness and desperation, Romeo's grief is much like Juliet's. His speech, like hers, echoes with doom hanging in the oft-repeated "banished." Like her, he is so beside himself with misery that he feels exile is death, and he even starts invoking death. Since the holy Friar is the opposite of the earthy, licentious Nurse, he tries to suppress the overwhelming emotions of Romeo by being direct, optimistic, and philosophical instead of indulging in emotional display by deceitfulness, pessimism, and sentiment. His effect on Romeo is similar to the Nurse's effect on Juliet: Both are goaded to an even more frantic distraction of grief. Romeo finally collapses on the floor.

The parallelism of this scene and the previous one is deliberate. It shows how similar are the passions of the lovers for each other. By contrasting the Nurse and the Friar, Shakespeare has made it clear that adults of the most widely differing temperaments and character-istics cannot understand this passion of young love. Whether self-indulgent or philosophical, old age is incapable of comprehension or even proper sympathy in this case. Romeo goes so far as to tell the Friar this. Again, the passion of love is kept aloft—isolated from age, from being temperate, and in fact, from the play itself.

The aloneness of the lovers is crystal clear. It is love alone that can direct their actions.

As Romeo throws himself to the floor in despair, there is a knocking at the Friar's door. The Friar is concerned at the idea of the young exile's being discovered. He tells Romeo to control himself and hide before he is found. Romeo refuses, saying that if his love hides him then he will be hidden. When the Friar finally gives up and asks who is there, we hear with relief the voice of the Nurse, saying that she comes on an errand for Juliet. The Friar is as relieved as the audience, and he lets the Nurse enter. When she sees Romeo lying on the ground in a fit of distracted grief, she declares that her mistress is in the same pitiful state, "weeping and blubber-ing." She tells Romeo that for Juliet's sake he must stand up like a man. To this persuasion Romeo responds and recovers himself. His first words are of Juliet: Does she think he is a murderer now that he has killed her cousin? Where is she? How is she? What is she thinking? The Nurse answers that Juliet only cries, falls on her bed, and calls out first Tybalt's name, then Romeo's. Romeo is afraid that his name will mean death to his young wife. He draws his sword, ready to plunge it into whatever part of his body houses his own name.

COMMENT

Romeo is still distraught, and he responds to the Nurse's indirect answer just as Juliet did: with a fervor of unhappiness and even an effort to kill himself. The Nurse is again savoring every drop of emotion that can be wrung from the scene, and again she is unintentionally cruel.

Seeing Romeo draw his sword is too much for the kind Friar. He jumps to prevent the act, and in doing so lets loose a torrent of invective at such impetuosity and, as it seems to him, lack of maturity in Romeo. "Art thou a man?" he asks. Romeo's form is a man's but his tears have been those of a woman and his acts those of a wild beast. The Friar is amazed; he had thought Romeo's disposition was "better tempered." So Romeo has killed Tybalt; does he now want to kill himself, and by doing so, kill Juliet too? The Friar declares that Romeo is shaming his own shape, love, and wit. When the Friar's speech reaches this point, his anger begins to subside and the philosophy he has been wanting to encourage replaces it. The Friar's language and the structure of his speech become more formal. Using the three aspects of shape, love, and wit, he cautions Romeo. The misuse of these three things in a man changes his shape into mere wax, lacking in manliness; his love into a lie that can only kill itself; and his wit into a blaze of ignorance. Romeo has been doing this to himself. But the Friar encourages his young friend also, reminding him to be happy: After all, Juliet is alive; Romeo himself, instead of being dead by Tybalt's sword, has killed his would-be killer; and the law that would have had him executed has softened and only exiled him. The Friar sees all this as a "pack of blessings," which Romeo mistakenly ignores. He warmly advises the young lover to go to his new wife, to comfort her, and only to be cautious and leave for the town of Mantua early enough to escape detection. Turning to the Nurse, the Friar sends her back to Juliet with the news that "Romeo is coming." The Nurse praises the Friar's good advice, and the Friar tells Romeo that he will find a time when he can joyfully call him back to a reconciled family, his marriage with Juliet, and a pardon from the Prince. The Nurse promises to deliver her message. Romeo, restored at the prospect of seeing Juliet, tells the Nurse that Juliet should prepare to "chide" him. He accepts the ring his beloved has sent, and as the Nurse bustles out, Romeo's "comfort is revived" by it. The Friar, feeling his old genial self again, says goodbye to Romeo, urging him to take care when leaving Verona. The Friar will keep him posted as to what is happening in his absence. Romeo, who values the Friar highly, leaves to go to his bride, saying, "But that a joy past joy calls out on me,/ It were a grief so brief to part with thee."

COMMENT

The disparity between youth and age is again empha-sized by the Friar's long philosophical speech, in which he advises Romeo to be careful and moderate. It is cautiously worded and formal. Even the Friar's initial anger is expressed in clear parallels and comparisons, and all his wisdom comes from temperance. He scolds Romeo for not being himself temperate, for the good Friar does not understand that being temperate is incompatible with Romeo's whole state of being at present. But it is not these balanced phrases about shape, love, and wit that cause the rise in Romeo's spirits. Instead, it is the Friar's urging that he go to Juliet imme-diately that prompts Romeo to regain himself. The threat of the feud and the sentence of exile are a heavy reminder in the Friar's warnings. The audience hears them, even if Romeo, in his joy, seems oblivious. When Romeo receives the ring, the scene comes full circle with its companion scene, in which Juliet sends the ring. We look forward to the joyful but secret consummation of the marriage.

SUMMARY

This scene has directly paralleled the preceding one, has

completed the preparations for the marriage night, and has heightened the foreboding tragedy by showing us Romeo's response to it. The Nurse and the Friar have been contrasted, and together they illustrate the incompatibility and lack of understanding between old age and youth. The impossibility of any meetings of the mind between the lovers and their confidants is clear, and the plot rushes forward as impetuously as the lovers themselves.

ACT III, SCENE 4

Abruptly we find ourselves at the Capulet house, where Lord and Lady Capulet are talking to Paris about his proposal of marriage to Juliet. Capulet explains that, due to the misfortune of Tybalt's death, they have had no time to pursue the matter of Juliet's marriage. She and her parents loved Tybalt, and Capulet sighs philosophically, "Well, we were born to die." Juliet will not be down tonight, and Lord and Lady Capulet themselves would have been in bed by now, if it were not for their visit with Paris. Paris is sympathetic to these things, and he prepares to take his leave. Lady Capulet promises to speak to her daughter about this marriage tomorrow, but her husband is even more eager to seal the match. He breaks in, saying that he feels he is on firm ground in promising Juliet's assent to the proposal: "I think she will be ruled/ In all respects by me." Turning to his wife, he tells Lady Capulet to go to Juliet tonight, immediately after Paris leaves, and tell her that Paris loves her and that she is to marry him.

COMMENT

Lord Capulet speaks in his usual relaxed way, but his attitude toward the proposed marriage has changed greatly. Whereas before he emphasized Juliet's youth and suggested that Paris wait a few years, but left the final word to his prized daughter, he now feels just the opposite. He wants this marriage to take place as soon as possible. He will tell Juliet she is getting married, not ask her opinion of the matter. He even calls Paris "my son," being so sure that his daughter will oblige him. This is not incompatible with his former characterization. Throughout the scenes in which he appears, and especially at his own party where he bosses the servants and scolds Tybalt for his outburst, he has shown himself to be conscious and proud of his role as lord of the household. He likes to think of himself as genial, liberal, and kindly, and he truly loves his daughter, for he first says that she alone can make the decision. But actually he allows no opposition to his will; and since he feels sure he knows what is best for his daughter, he now promises for her. There is some psychological justification, also, for his change of heart. More feuding has added to the old disfavor of his family among the people of Verona, and his own Tybalt has killed a relative of the Prince. This is the apt and politic time for Capulet to restore his good name by marrying his only daughter to another of the Prince's relatives. Besides, Paris is a good match, both noble and rich.

Lord Capulet is eager to have the marriage as soon as the proper time for grief has elapsed. He settles on Thursday, three days from now, and he hopes that Paris will approve of this haste. In view of Tybalt's recent death, and so that no one will think his own family didn't love him, the wedding will be kept small and sober, with only a few guests. Paris agrees to all this readily; for him, tomorrow would not be too soon. Everything settled, Capulet calls for a servant to light his way to bed and tells his wife to give Juliet the news and prepare her for the marriage. With a comment that it is so late it might even be called early morning, he bids "Goodnight."

COMMENT

Our impression of Lord Capulet's haste is reinforced; and this, added to the shortness of the scene, strengthens our own feeling of the speed of the plot. There is added irony in the fact that we know that Juliet is married already. She is not mourning for Tybalt, as her parents suppose, nor is she expecting such news as this. She is with her new husband now. Capulet's last remark about whether to call the time late night or early morning leads directly and ironically to the next scene, where the parting couple do call it early, and feel it to be too early to part.

SUMMARY

This short, quick scene, falling as it does between the preparations for the lovers' wedding night and their leave-taking after their night together, has more than one effect:

(1) By setting a wedding date only three days off, it enhances both the speed of the action and our feeling of the necessity for speed.

(2) It strikes us with the bitter irony of preparing for a marriage when we know that one already has taken place and is now being consummated. Romeo's banishment is tragic news, but it is an irony of fate that the threat of this other marriage is partially caused by the same incident.

(3) We are impressed more strongly than ever with the doom that overhangs the love of Romeo and Juliet.

ACT III, SCENE 5

It is Capulet's orchard at night. Again we find Juliet high aloft on her balcony, with the light from the room behind her setting her off. But this time, Romeo is not below her; he stands with her on the balcony. They have spent one glorious night together, but the time has come for them to part and for Romeo to go into exile. As the scene opens, Romeo apparently has begun to take his leave, and the first words we hear are Juliet's "Wilt thou be gone? It is not yet near day." The lovers have heard a bird singing. Juliet says that it is the nightingale, a bird known for serenading in the night. She denies that it is the lark, a bird that sings at the break of day, and insists sweetly on the fact that there is a nightingale in her garden who sings each night from a certain tree, saying it was his call they heard. She wants Romeo to believe her so that he will not leave yet. But Romeo knows "It was the lark, the herald of the morn," and he points to the malicious light that is beginning to cut through the clouds in the east, where the sun will rise. "Night's candles are burnt out," he says, "and jocund [jolly] day/ stands tiptoe on the misty mountain tops:/ I must be gone and live, or stay and die." Despite his consciousness of the anguish of departure and the sure death that will find him if he stays, Romeo's images are permeated with the joy of the night he has just spent. Juliet refuses to recognize what she knows to be true. She hopefully insists that the light is a meteor sent as a torch to guide Romeo to Mantua and that he can linger still a while longer.

COMMENT

We have waited for this scene with high anticipation, through the past three scenes; to have it begin with the parting of the lovers, however ecstatic, increases the sense of joy as being fleeting, and of the need for haste. The orchard we connect vividly with the first sweet wooing and parting of the lovers, only one night previous, and it is the perfect place for this scene. Perfect, also, is the vision of Romeo and Juliet, now married in soul and in body, standing together on the lighted balcony, where before they were separate. The images of night and darkness as being welcome and joyful, and of the light of day as bringing threats of separation, of making dim the light of love that glows brightly at night, are better developed than ever. The bird they love sings at night, the light of dawn is malicious, and the meteor, mentioned by Juliet, is like an image of their love: a miraculous and sudden brilliance in the dark heavens that dies out too soon.

Romeo is vulnerable to the persuasions of his beloved. He will stay and be put to death if she wishes. He will say that the grey of dawn is only a reflection of the moon (Cynthia), and that the calling of that bird in the sky is not that of the lark. "I have more care to stay than will to go," he says, and he welcomes death because Juliet seems to prefer it to parting. But Juliet does not want him to die, and she immediately changes her tune, says that it is day and that he must leave quickly. That bird is the lark; but instead of making "sweet division" (that is, singing a series of short lyric notes instead of one long one) its song seems to her to be "harsh discords" because it pronounces the "division" of herself from Romeo. As the lark "hunts up" (arouses) the day, so it hunts Romeo out of town and away from her. The light of dawn increases as she speaks, and she wails, "O now be gone; more light and light it grows." Romeo answers, "More light and light, more dark and dark our woes!" The Nurse entering Juliet's room (from which they are curtained off as they stand on the balcony) interrupts gruffly with "Madam." She warns that Juliet's mother is coming to her room, and adds, "The day is broke; be wary, look about." Juliet can only answer in dismay, "Then window, let day in, and let life out." Romeo kisses her and then climbs down from the balcony.

COMMENT

That Romeo would stay and die if Juliet preferred, we must believe. He has just spent a night of the highest joy he has ever known, and even death seems slight beside it, especially if Juliet prefers it. But she hopes for more such joy, so she wants to live. Daylight, however, brings with it cruel revealing lights that force unpleasant realities on these lovers, who are infused with the darkness of their night together and the brightness of their love. The most unpleasant reality is their parting. As the light increases, the darkness of the pain of parting to which they must submit also increases. They feel this strongly, and so hate the light, as is clear in Juliet's outpourings against the lark, and in Romeo's cry of their darkening woe. The cruel reality of day and the necessity for caution is finally brought home to them by the Nurse. She represents to the lovers the lack of understanding of the outside world, the reality of the baser side of life, and an old age that forever advises caution. Her voice and words grate across their duet unpleasantly but seal the facts they must face in the hated daylight. She begins the lovers' leave-taking.

The benevolence of night and the menace of light is carried still further in both the images of speech and the actions of the lovers. Daylight means not only darkening woe but, as we see in Juliet's last words, death. The lovers live in darkness; the day and the parting seem to make the life of their love impossible, seem to threaten to replace their love in darkness with the eternal darkness of death. The imagery of light and dark, so played upon their courting, has begun to take shape and affect the action. Evil, fate, the realities and cautions of old age, and the outside world are all becoming connected with the daytime. Love is possible only at night, and stands opposed to all other elements in the play.

The lovers part. Juliet, calling to her "love-lord" and "husband-friend," begs that she hear often from him, for in the space of a minute of their separation, days will seem to pass. Romeo assures her that he will let no chance of sending her news escape him. He is sure they will be together again, to talk over joyfully the pains of their separation. But even as he says this, Juliet is startled by what seems an evil vision. As she looks down at him in the grey light below, he seems to resemble a corpse, and she cries: "O God! I have an ill-divining soul:/ Methinks I see thee, now thou art below,/ As one dead at the bottom of a tomb." Romeo, seeing her pallor, has the same sensation, but he comforts her by saying, "Dry sorrow drinks our blood," meaning that their sadness at parting has drawn the blood from their faces. Calling "Adieu," he leaves quickly.

COMMENT

This final parting is full of ill-omen. The lovers' promises to send messages back and forth are ironic, as we know if we have read the play before, for it is the failure of a message to reach its destination that precipitates their tragedy. The mutual vision of the lovers, seeing each other dead and cold in a tomb, is starkly prophetic. That is exactly how and when they will meet again.

As Romeo disappears into the growing morning, Juliet speaks of fortune, hoping that it will be as fickle as people say it is, for then it will turn the misfortune of this parting back to good fortune, and the lovers will be together again. Just then, Lady Capulet enters. Juliet, wondering what unusual happening causes her mother to be up this late or to have arisen this early, goes in to her. Seeing her daughter's tear-stained face, Lady Capulet expresses surprise. When Juliet claims not to be feeling well, the Lady, assuming that the tears have been shed over Tybalt's death, chides her daughter. Even if she washed her cousin's grave with tears, she could not make him alive, and while much grief indicates great love, too much grieving is a sign of stupidity. Juliet takes up this cue as a way to keep her secret from her mother and still not have to restrain her own excessive feeling of grief at parting from Romeo. She speaks on two levels, and referring within herself to Romeo, she says, "Yet let me weep for such a feeling loss." Trying to console her daughter, Lady Capulet says she should try to feel her friendship for Tybalt, not her loss. If Juliet must cry, it should be over the fact that the man who killed Tybalt is alive. Juliet, sensing fully the irony of this conversation, whispers to herself that she pardons that man, and yet no man gives her more grief. Overhearing the last of this, the Lady says that of course Juliet grieves that the murderer lives, to which Juliet replies ironically that her grief is that he lives too far from her hands. Then, fearing that she will be discovered in her word-tricks, she adds what her mother assumed she meant, that she wants vengeance. To soothe the girl, Lady

Capulet promises to send someone to Mantua to poison Romeo. At this Juliet is frightened, but replies with great presence of mind, that if this is to be done, she must "temper" the poison. She means, of course, not to make it stronger, but to make it completely ineffectual. She goes so far as to say that she can't bear to hear Romeo named, when she cannot even go to him and "Wreak the love I bore my cousin Tybalt/ Upon his body." She truly means "love," but again her mother assumes she means revenge. But the Lady's visit has another purpose; she changes the subject, saying she brings "joyful tidings," and Juliet answers that she needs some joyous news.

COMMENT

Juliet's wondering as to why her mother comes so early or late hearkens back to Capulet's last words at the end of the scene in which he promised Juliet in marriage to Paris, and made plans for a quick wedding. So we are reminded of Lady Capulet's errand, and the irony of it hangs like a sword over the already ironic scene. Juliet is still in great sorrow for Romeo. The cleverness with which she covers over the tears she cannot hold back, attributing them to Tybalt's death and convincing her own mother, makes us again aware of how rapidly she is becoming an adult and a woman. The double meaning of all her words about Romeo keeps our interest, and both Juliet and the audience take a certain pleasure in this bitter audacity. The scene is a study in dramatic irony. Even the reference to poison is, as we will discover, ironic and foreboding.

Lady Capulet tells Juliet that her father, out of concern for her grief, has arranged for her an especially happy day in the near future: On Thursday she is to marry the gallant young nobleman, Paris. Juliet retorts abruptly that Paris will not make her into a joyful bride, but she covers herself by protesting at this haste in the midst of Tybalt's loss and at being married without even being courted. She swears she will not marry—and to make her mother feel the finality of this as well as to give vent to her feelings, she swears she'll first marry Romeo (whom they know she hates). At this point, Lord Capulet comes himself, with the Nurse, to see how his daughter responds. He is in high spirits, and makes jokes about the dew, the rain, the shower of tears his daughter has cried out. He compares Juliet to a ship in the midst of a storm, shaking her own body with winds of sighing and tides of crying. He turns to ask his wife if she has delivered "our decree," and Lady Capulet tells him of Juliet's refusal, adding, "I would the fool were married to her grave." Capulet can't believe his ears; he asks if Juliet is not thankful, proud, and blessed to be given such a husband. Juliet answers that she is not proud of what she hates, but she is thankful to her parents even for this hateful thing they have done out of love for her. Capulet is extremely irritated. He calls his daughter's answer "chop-logic," a mere bargaining with twisted logic. He imitates her manner offensively. Growing more infuriated as he speaks, the Lord says, "Thank me no thankings, nor proud me no prouds," meaning he will have none of either. Ranting, he declares in vivid language that Juliet will dress and get herself to Paris at the church on Thursday, or he will drag her there. By this time he is beside himself with rage at being opposed by Juliet; referring to her great pallor, he calls her a waxy-faced "baggage," another word for a slut. At this, both Juliet and her mother call out in protest, but Capulet is going full blast. He repeats his demand that Juliet marry on Thursday, making it an ultimatum by adding that if she doesn't, he'll never look at her again. He wants no answers; in his rage his fingers itch to slap his daughter, and he calls her a curse on his life.

COMMENT

Lady Capulet sincerely believes she is bringing happy news. Indeed, we of the audience have every reason to believe that under other circumstances, Paris would have made an excellent, loving husband for Juliet. But we share with Juliet the irony of this "happiness" she is offered. She is shocked, and her abrupt refusal is understandable, but with an adult instinct for self-preservation she covers her feelings quickly, using more words of double meaning. Her mother's remark in response to this refusal that she'd rather have Juliet "married to her grave" rings not only an ironic but a fateful tone. Part of the irony of this scene has been its comparative calmness, and all these layers of irony are finally broken by Lord Capulet's utter fury. This aspect of his temperament has been established in a milder way by his outburst when Tybalt began to start a fight at the Capulet feast. We now see Capulet in full. He is old, testy, and not to be crossed. Capulet is lenient only when it suits him. We have seen that he has his reasons for wanting this marriage immediately, and it does not suit him to be lenient now. His anger, expressed as always in his loose, colorful, and direct language, has been prepared for throughout the scenes in which he has appeared.

Lady Capulet and Juliet can offer no retort to the Lord's stream of invective. It is the Nurse who breaks in and tells him he must blame himself for so losing his temper. He snaps back sarcastically, suggesting that "my lady wisdom" save her tongue for gossiping. The Nurse persists, and when Capulet calls her a "mumbling fool," Lady Capulet at last finds words. "You are too hot," she says. His anger subsiding only a bit, the Lord finds he must defend his rashness. He says he has thought much about whom he will match with his only daughter, and now he has found the perfect match, a man against whom no objections can be made. After all this, he cannot abide his daughter, "wretched, puling fool," having the nerve and stupidity to say no. With menace but comparative calm, he delivers his last word: Juliet may think it over, but if by Thursday she still refuses to marry, he will turn her out of house and home forever and let her "Hang, beg, starve, die in the streets." This is his final warning, and he leaves.

COMMENT

It is significant that only the realistic and plain-spoken Nurse, who is surely the gossip Capulet calls her, can interrupt his ranting, and that she does so to accuse the Lord straight-out of being unfair. Even though he is annoyed at this, Capulet senses her justice. He calms down enough to explain his anger and to deliver with more deliberation his ultimatum. His speech retains its vigor and slanginess, but it is not so vulgar. By the time he exits, we firmly believe that he has set his mind on this and will not be swayed. How his already secretly married daughter will manage, we cannot think.

Juliet begs for pity—first from the clouds, then from her mother. If the marriage cannot be delayed for a month or a week, Juliet asks that they "make the bridal bed in that dim monument where Tybalt lies." But Lady Capulet refuses even to discuss the matter; she leaves as abruptly as her husband did. Clearly, the marriage must be prevented. Juliet is caught: Her husband is alive on earth, and her religious faith forbids her to have two husbands. She cannot break such a stern law of the Church, but the only way she can see of preventing such a sin is for Romeo himself to die, leave earth, and go to heaven. The misery of such a prospect, and indeed of all that lies before Juliet, makes her turn and beg for comfort from her Nurse. The Nurse has only one solution. Since Romeo is banished, it is unlikely that he would return to challenge Juliet's marriage to Paris; and even if he dared, he could not do it openly. Considering this, the Nurse gently advises her mistress to marry Paris. She begins to extol Paris's virtues, calling him an eagle, he is so quick and handsome. She calls Romeo a "dishclout," meaning he can't compare with Paris, and she says that this second marriage will be better than the first. Even if Juliet doesn't agree to this comparison of the two, the Nurse thinks Romeo as good as dead, being permanently absent, and therefore of no use to Juliet. Juliet, astounded, asks the Nurse if she means this. The Nurse curses herself if she doesn't. Juliet's answer, "Amen," indicates that she too curses the Nurse for these thoughts. But she only says mildly that she is comforted and that she will now go alone to Friar Laurence, where she will make her confession to having displeased her father. The Nurse goes to tell Lady Capulet this encouraging news. The moment she is out of sight, Juliet bursts forth, "Ancient damnation! O most wicked fiend." She curses the Nurse furiously and cannot even decide whether the Nurse sins more in suggesting that she have two husbands, or in hypocritically degrading the Romeo she has so often highly praised. She severs herself forever from the Nurse: "Go counsellor;/ Thou and my bosom henceforth shall be twain." She resolves to go to the Friar for advice—and if he can give none, to find the strength to die.

COMMENT

Juliet is truly caught between heaven and earth. All her choices offer only evil and misery. She even goes so far as to ask to be put in the tomb with Tybalt rather than marry on Thursday. She does not know how close this request comes to what actually will occur. When she goes to her old Nurse for comfort, that Nurse, who truly cares for her mistress, does her best. But she sees the problem in a different light, resulting in a very base, unpleasantly realistic response. To her, hypocrisy and bigamy need not be sinful; they may be the only natural course, the only path to a happy life. This is not only old age speaking; the Nurse's opinion on the problem affirms life as she sees it, and as we know it in her by her vigor: long, pleasurable, and without conscience. To Juliet, such an attitude is horrid and repugnant beyond comprehension. She is young, fervently in love, and of a religious and idealistic mind. She would no sooner be unfaithful to her husband than she would break the decrees of heaven. The Nurse's way seems to offer not a pleasant and easy life, but misery, self-hatred, and torture. So she curses her old confidante and cuts her off, although her canny and adult instinct for self-preservation allows her to mask her response with hypocrisy. She is now alienated from all the world but her love, Romeo, and her religion, represented by the Friar. This alienation, coupled with her predicament and the passion of a young girl in love with all the depth of her self and her imagination, ends the scene on a fierce and ominous note. We believe she will find the strength to die, if the Friar cannot help her.

SUMMARY

The scene is a long and complex one, but through it are established the following:

(1) The images of love-provoking night and love-dispelling day have gathered potency and have begun even to affect the action. Day has come to mean all the harsh realities that threaten the lovers. Day looms almost as large as the fate that propels the action. Even though love prospers only at night, its impetuosity lends greater speed to the fateful direction of the plot.

(2) Accident and circumstance, in the form of the double killing of Mercutio and Tybalt, already have put great opposition in the lovers' way by resulting in the banishment of Romeo. They now add another stumbling-block: Lord Capulet's unrelenting insistence on Juliet's immediate marriage to Paris. This insistence not only puts another obstacle before the lovers but adds a sense of the necessity of still greater speed. In these many repercussions, we see clearly that the duels at the beginning of the act were fateful.

(3) The characters of Lord Capulet and the Nurse are rounded out—and are now totally alien to Juliet. She herself shows new strength and growth in her ironic handling of her own grief when faced with her mother and in the subtle retraction by which she pretends to agree with the Nurse. There is a

female capacity for necessary deception here, but it leaves her completely alone. She has no one with whom to share secrets, and she must stand on her own two feet.

(4) Irony plays a larger part than ever, as the plot becomes more complicated and the strands of action interweave.

Act III has reached its culmination. The play's initial turn to tragedy, with the deaths of Mercutio and Tybalt, took place in the first scene. The result for the two lovers was Romeo's exile and a repetition of the threat of the feud. Romeo and Juliet's grief at this banishment and their anticipation of the night together have been fully realized in their loving leave-taking. The feud asserts itself again as the reason for Capulet's insistence on Juliet's marrying Paris. The act closes with Romeo off alone in Mantua, Juliet an alien in her own house, and the additional obstacle of another marriage threatening the lovers.

ROMEO AND JULIET
ACT IV

ACT IV, SCENE 1

The act opens, as we might have expected, in Friar Laurence's cell. But it is Paris, not Juliet, who is visiting the good Friar. Apparently, Paris has asked him to perform the coming marriage between himself and Juliet. The Friar realizes as fully as we do the dangerous implications of such a union. His first words are full of perplexity and hesitation: "On Thursday, sir? the time is very short." Paris answers that this speed is Capulet's wish, and that he, too, is eager to marry soon. The Friar then raises the objection that Juliet has not yet given her consent, but Paris can explain that also. He did not wish to speak of love in a house full of grief, and Lord Capulet urges the speedy marriage specifically so that his daughter will not mourn herself into oblivion over Tybalt. The Friar mutters to himself that he wishes he could think of a reason—one that he was free to tell—that would explain why this marriage should be put off.

COMMENT

The Friar, who has all along objected to hastiness as immoderate, now finds himself objecting again. This time, however, he has a reason: the completed marriage of Romeo and Juliet, about which he is not at liberty to speak. So he hesitates, and defers decision. In this hesitation, we begin to see the Friar's fault. Perhaps he should go directly to Capulet and tell him outright of the marriage. Once again, the speed of the action appears as inevitable and fateful.

At this point, Juliet arrives at the cell. Paris greets her as "my lady and my wife"; and although Juliet must be taken aback to see him, she answers demurely, "That may be, sir, when I may be a wife." Paris says she shall be his wife, as of Thursday, to which Juliet makes a noncommittal but assenting reply. Their conversation proceeds in single-line remarks and replies. Paris pressures her to declare her love for him, but she sidesteps his efforts with coy modesty. When Paris comments that her face is abused with tears, she answers that her face was bad enough before the tears. When he admonishes her not to slander her face, for it is now his, she only replies cryptically that perhaps it is his; at any rate, it is not hers. What she means is that it belongs to Romeo. To escape further conversation, she turns to the Friar and asks if she may see him now or if she should come later. The Friar asks Paris to leave them alone; he does so, but not before promising to come for Juliet early Thursday and taking a parting kiss as he goes. When she is alone with the Friar at last, Juliet's composure crumbles, and she breaks into cries of grief. The Friar tries to comfort her, saying that he knows what has happened and that it strains his wits to fully grasp the awfulness of it. Juliet wants only to know how to prevent the marriage. If the Friar has no answer, she only asks his blessing on her suicide. Her hand and heart have been joined to Romeo's in holy wedlock, as the Friar knows. Before her hand could clasp another's or her heart perform such treachery as another marriage, she would use her dagger to end the life in both hand and heart. Can the Friar restore her to true honor? She urges him to answer; if he cannot, she will kill herself.

COMMENT

The reserve and caution with which Juliet responds to Paris is commendable. She does not let him think her unwilling, lest he go to question her father; nor is she ever in the smallest gesture or word untrue to Romeo. Paris exerts some degree of pressure on her, calling her his love and kissing her. It is not surprising that she loses all control as soon as she is alone with the Friar. Her speech deals with the hands and heart by which she pledged herself to Romeo, but there are no pretty images here. Her language is plain, for she is in deadly earnest and would willingly kill herself with a dagger if there were no help for this situation. She is impassioned with grief now, even more impetuous than before. Nor is it the last time we will see her ominous dagger.

The Friar quiets her, for he sees some hope. It is a desperate hope; but in the face of the threat of another marriage, it is better than none. If Juliet is desperate enough to kill herself, perhaps she will be willing to undergo something very close to death, but not death itself, which could free her from her shame. Juliet is all eagerness, declaring she would jump off a battlement, go among thieves and serpents, be chained among bears, and even allow herself to be shut into a sepulchre of the dead (a "charnel-house"). On this last her headstrong imagination catches, for it holds the greatest horror. She says she would let herself be covered with stinking, rattling, yellow bones, or even hide in the shroud of a newly dead man. She has trembled at hearing her own descriptions, but she would do any of these, "Without fear or doubt, To live an unstain'd wife" to Romeo.

COMMENT

The Friar's yet unspoken plan, which offers some hope for Juliet to live and be true to her lover, involves undergoing something similar to death. Juliet, who loves Romeo with the full force of her being, seizes on even the faintest hope. Her charged imagination runs riot among all the horrors she can conceive that she would endure for the sake of this hope. She dwells longest on going into a house of the dead and associating with the corpses there. What she does not know is that something of exactly this nature will be required of her: She will have to seem to die, and be buried, in order to live.

The Friar, convinced by Juliet's desperation that she has the strength to do this, begins slowly to outline his plan. She is to go home, act cheerful, and pretend to agree to the marriage. Tomorrow night, Wednesday, the night before the wedding, she is to get into bed and drink the liquid from a small vial, or container, which the Friar will give her. She will feel her veins grow cold, and her pulse will slow to a standstill. She will sleep—cold, pale, and without breath—and it will be a sleep "Like death, when he shuts up the day of life," stiff and corpselike. This will last forty-two hours, and then she will awaken pleasantly. In the meantime, Paris will find her and think her dead; and as is customary, she will be placed in full dress on an open bier or platform and taken to the Capulet family tomb. While this happens, the Friar will send letters of explanation to Romeo, who will come to Verona and meet the Friar. When Juliet awakens, they will be at her side. Then Romeo will take Juliet with him to Mantua, and she will be free from shame. The Friar only hopes that she will not lose her valor and be afraid to take the drug. Juliet responds, "Give me, give me!" The Friar gives her the little flask and wishes her well, promising to send to Romeo immediately. "Love give me strength! and strength shall help afford" are Juliet's words as she leaves the Friar's cell.

COMMENT

We know the Friar is educated in the lore of herbs and potions. We scarcely doubt that this liquid of his will perform as he says it will. As always, the Friar's tone is rational and cautious. He is doing his best to help Juliet; still, the prospect of this temporary death is chilling, like a wind foreboding evil. It is too much like real death, of which there has been sufficient warning, and we wonder if all this connivance and deceit are necessary. The audience, along with Juliet, accepts the Friar's plan, but not without a premonition of dread and a shudder.

SUMMARY

The necessity for some quick action is apparent, as the marriage of Juliet to Paris already has reached the stage of concrete preparations for the ceremony. Juliet threatens to kill herself and later imagines vividly all the horrors of a tomb, full of rotting bodies. Finally, the only hope lies in a kind of temporary death, induced by the Friar's drug. The theme of death, ominously hinted at in earlier scenes, now is presented fully and occupies an entire scene. The lovers' only hope lies in death of a temporary nature. This brings to mind how, throughout the play, night and darkness, which are parallel to death, have been the lovers' only source of joy.

ACT IV, SCENE 2

The scene is the Capulet house, where the mood is merry, in contrast to the previous one. Capulet sends out one servant with a list of guests to be invited to the wedding feast and another to fetch twenty cooks. The Nurse tells Capulet that Juliet is with the Friar, and he comments that he hopes the visit will do his peevish, self-willed daughter some good. Juliet appears at that moment, and the Nurse notices that she looks merry. "How now, my headstrong! where have you been gadding?" calls her father in jolly tones. Juliet answers that she has repented her opposition to him, and has been told by the Friar to beg her father's pardon. She does so now, with a nice gesture. At this Lord Capulet is delighted, sends out a servant to tell Paris, and decides to hold the wedding the next day—Wednesday, instead of Thursday, as was planned.

COMMENT

The scene does seem bustling and jovial; but our knowledge of the situation, the desperate plan under way, and Juliet's deception dim the atmosphere. Capulet, who loves his daughter, is genuinely and heartily glad to see her; he even teases her at being willful before he knows for sure that she has changed her mind to suit his will. When she apologizes, he is so pleased that he makes plans to have the wedding a day earlier. At this, we feel a certain dread, knowing the exactness of the Friar's timing.

Juliet tells her father how she met Paris at the Friar's and gave him as much love as her modesty would allow. Capulet is even more pleased. Now he wants Paris brought to him, and praises the Friar for having so well directed his daughter. Juliet goes off with the Nurse to prepare clothing for the wedding. When Lady Capulet protests that they cannot be ready by tomorrow, Capulet says he'll handle things. His wife may go help Juliet; he intends to stay up all night and even play house-wife. He calls for a servant; then, realizing that they are all running errands, he decides to go himself to see Paris and prepare him for the wedding. His heart is "wondrous light," now that his wayward Juliet has come back to him.

COMMENT

The light mood continues to be ironic. This happiness that Lord Capulet feels at his daughter's giving in to him is pitiable, in view of what we know is to happen. Moving the marriage up one day is done by the Lord in happy haste. Ironically, this will only hasten Capulet's own grief. The speed of the plot has been increased by this whim of old Capulet; and as the action hurries forward, the feeling of fatefulness and evil doom grows with it. Under the surface of this upbeat interlude, another threat has materialized. Perhaps Juliet, in her great desire to be convincing and so preserve herself for Romeo, has played her part too well.

ACT IV, SCENE 3

In her bedroom, Juliet and her Nurse have finished preparing the dress she will wear tomorrow. Juliet asks that the Nurse leave her alone tonight; she pleads that she has many prayers ("orisons") to make, so that heaven will forgive the sinfulness she is about to begin. Lady Capulet comes to offer help, but Juliet has nothing more to do. She asks her mother to take the Nurse, who could help the Lady with her own preparations, as Juliet wishes to be alone. Telling the young girl to rest well, the Nurse and Lady Capulet leave.

COMMENT

Juliet has carefully contrived to be alone, as she plans to take the Friar's drug. She will rest more deeply and longer than the Nurse and Lady Capulet suspect.

"God knows when she shall meet again," Juliet says to herself as her Nurse and Mother depart. She faces a great trial, and although she feels alien to them, she is not sure when she will again see any humans at all. Already, fear makes her blood run cold, and she cannot feel the heat of her own life. She is tempted, and starts to call the Nurse back for comfort. But there is nothing the Nurse can do to help: "My dismal scene I needs must act alone." She considers the flask of liquid— "Come vial"—and wonders what will happen if the drug does not work. She will not marry, and to assure herself of that she puts her dagger within easy reach. Again she questions, fearfully, whether perhaps the Friar has not given her real poison, to avoid the dishonor that would fall on him if it became known that he had performed her marriage to Romeo. She fears this, but she knows better, for the Friar has always proved himself a holy individual.

COMMENT

Juliet now has come face to face with the taking of the potion. She is very much alone. She fears the deed, for she is about to submit herself to the unknown. Her fear is first, that the liquid will not work; then, that it will work too well. But she masters both these feelings, explaining them away as most unlikely.

Yet another fear occurs to the young girl—the fear that she will wake in the tomb too early, before Romeo comes to "redeem" her. This she accepts as a justified fear, and she begins to imagine herself stifling and suffocating in the foul air of the vault, and dying of slow strangulation before Romeo arrives. And if she doesn't die for lack of air? If she lives, she will find herself in the midst of night, death, and the terror of "an ancient receptacle," containing the bones of ancestors hundreds of years old, "Where bloody Tybalt, yet but green in earth,/ Lies festering in his shroud." This image of decaying flesh brings to her mind a worse terror, that of the undead spirits whom she has heard frequent tombs of the dead. Juliet's imagination races and riots with these dreadful visions; she sees herself, waking early to hideous odors and "shrieks like mandrakes torn out of the earth." (Mandrakes were roots grown from the bodies of criminals who had been executed and buried; when torn up, they were supposed to omit wild shrieks that would drive insane whoever uprooted them.) Picturing this, she sees herself driven distraught with fear, playing madly with the bones of her ancestors; pulling Tybalt's mangled body from beneath his shroud; and finally, in crazed desperation, knocking out her own brains with some old bone. Wrought to a pitch of terror by her own frightened imaginings, Juliet now thinks she sees Tybalt's ghost vengefully attacking Romeo, his killer. She tries to stop the ghost, she seems to fail, and in her frenzy, she believes Romeo to have been killed. Without another thought, she swallows all the potion and tries to join her Romeo in death, crying, "Romeo, I come! This do I drink to thee." Juliet now falls, senseless, on her bed.

COMMENT

Juliet, overcome with the horrors of waking alone in a death-filled tomb, finally has succeeded in drinking the liquid in which lie both her hope and her fear. Her speech is a series of images increasing steadily in frenzy and horror; finally she envisions the thing she fears most, Romeo's death, and finds in her desire to be with him the strength to drink. That she is able to drink at all is a tribute to her character. Being alive among the dead was the thought that prevented her. Death itself holds no such fears, if in death she joins her love. In drinking the liquid, Juliet believes momentarily that she is joining Romeo in eternity, an idea that is to develop into a major theme. She celebrates this by drinking a toast to her lover. Romeo later makes the same gesture of a toast when, drinking poison, he joins her in death. In a sense, Juliet's taking of the potion is a symbolic suicide. The scene itself abounds with evil omens of death to come. But death is not so bad as living among the dead, or as living without love.

ACT IV, SCENE 4

It is early morning now, and the Capulet household is alive with the bustle of wedding preparations. The Nurse is sent to get spices. Dates and quinces are needed. Capulet is going about, arousing all those not yet busy and making sure no cost is spared on the baked meats. The Nurse scolds him playfully, calling him "cot-queen," a derogatory term for a man who is acting as a housewife, and telling him to get some rest. Lord Capulet refuses to sleep, saying he has been up all night before with less reason. Even Lady Capulet is in good spirits, and says his previous all-night vigils were mouse-hunts (chases after women). Capulet only ribs her in turn for being jealous.

COMMENT

The household as yet is unaware of what awaits them in Juliet's room. Their gaiety holds much irony for us, especially after the desperate scene just witnessed. The low-life, bawdy jocularity of all three major figures enhances the difference between them and the lovers and rubs salt in the wound they have not yet discovered.

Servants go to and fro, one with something the cook needs, another in search of dry logs. When Lord Capulet hurries them, they make jokes for his benefit. He awaits Paris, who will come with the musicians. Presently music is heard, and Capulet calls the Nurse. She must go wake Juliet and dress her properly while the Lord chats with the bridegroom. Capulet calls, "Make haste, I say."

COMMENT

Like the previous scene of bustle, this interlude is ironic
in mood. But it serves to mark time and to create an
atmosphere of haste and anticipation. It modulates the
pace of the action while increasing our impression of
unavoidable and necessary speed. With music, glad cries,
and haste, the next scene is ushered in.

ACT IV, SCENE 5

We come, with the Nurse, to Juliet's chamber. Juliet lies
hidden from sight on the curtained bed. Calling and scolding
cheerfully, the Nurse bustles about, perhaps drawing the
curtains from the windows. She believes her mistress is fast
asleep in bed, and as the Nurse hurries around she tries to
rouse Juliet with cries of, "lamb," "lady," "slug-a-bed," and
"bride." She admits that Juliet has need of a bit of sleep now,
for surely Paris plans to keep her sleepless these coming nights.
Still, she is surprised that Juliet sleeps so deeply, and finally
the Nurse is moved to pull the curtains of the bed apart. There
lies Juliet, fully dressed, which seems strange. The Nurse starts
to shake her, but the body beneath her hands feels stiff and
chill. Horrified, the Nurse wails, "Lady! Lady! Lady!" and "Help,
help! my lady's dead," in a crescendo of despair. Lady Capulet,
hearing this commotion, comes in quickly to see what is the
matter. The Nurse can only point and cry, "O lamentable day!"
and "O heavy day!" Seeing for herself how her daughter lies,
Lady Capulet moans, "My child, my only life,/ Revive, look
up, or I will die with thee," and calls for help. Now comes
Lord Capulet. Paris is waiting, and the Lord, annoyed at this
delay, has come to see that his daughter comes quickly. He is
greeted by both his wife and the Nurse, crying the word "dead"
over and over. His first reaction is close to anger: "Ha! let me
see her. Out, alas!" He feels how cold and stiff she is, and sees
how pale, and it seems to him that death has come "like an
untimely frost" to this sweet flower. The Lady and the Nurse
can say little; they mourn the sadness of this day and time.
And for the first time, Capulet himself can find no words, not
even a wail, for death "Ties up my tongue."

COMMENT

Juliet is not dead; but her deathlike sleep is totally convincing, and Nurse, mother, and father are all stricken. The only words they can find to express their grief are "dead," "day," and "time" or "untimely." They blame the day and the time, as the lovers have done, for their misfortune. It is not only her death that strikes them; it is the untimeliness of it. It comes too soon, for she was too young, and too many things awaited her in life. In fact, it is the speed of this that shocks them all speechless. The fateful speed that has compelled the action now strikes a blow.

Hurrying in come the Friar and Paris with the bridal musicians. The Friar asks, "Is the bride ready to go to church?" This prompts Capulet to regain his words; she is ready, he says, to go to church and never return. On the eve of the wedding, Death has slept with Paris's bride, and she, the flower, lies deflowered (robbed of her virginity) by death. It is Death who has married Juliet and is now Capulet's son-in-law and heir. Capulet can only die and leave all he has, including life, to Death. Paris, for whom this day promised much, stands bewildered. Lady Capulet now curses the day, this miserable hour in the pilgrimage of time, for having taken her one poor cause for joy out of life. The talkative Nurse finds no coherent thought, and only can curse repeatedly the black day, the hateful day. Now Paris finds words: He has been divorced by death, and now can love only in death. And again Lord Capulet cries out. His child was his soul; his soul lies martyred, and all joy is dead for him.

COMMENT

There is little differentiation, if any, among the expressions of grief by these very different characters. Their mourning makes one long, repetitive incantation of sorrow. It is more like a chorus than like individual voices, and the chorus comes in response to Lord Capulet's single, distinctive speech on Juliet's marriage to Death. It is as it this speech has summed up and given expression to all the bitterness and bereavement they feel. The join in chorus to give witness and affirmation to that speech. The chorus emphasizes once again how each person blames the day, the time, the untimeliness, and the speed with which death has come.

This scene and these indistinct, unindividualized expressions of grief will stand in sharp contrast to Romeo's reaction to the same news. The grief of the parents and fiance is no less real, but its amorphous quality differs greatly from the strength and poetic defiance it will find in the grief of Juliet's husband and lover. The meeting of death and marriage will also grow in meaning as we near the end of the play.

Knowing the true state of things, the Friar has retained his composure. He interrupts them now and tries to calm their grief with chiding philosophy: "Peace, ho! for shame! confusion's cure lives not/ In these confusions." He explains that these friends and relatives shared Juliet with heaven, and now heaven has all of her, and keeps her from death by giving her eternal life. This is an honor and a joy far greater than any of them could have offered her, and they are selfish not to be happy for her sake. He adds, "She's not well married that lives married long,/ But she's best married that dies married young." Juliet had once kept rosemary for Romeo (act II, scene 4, lines 217–218), and this evergreen herb, symbolizing eternal life and remembrance, was used at both weddings and funerals. Appropriately, the Friar mentions the herb now, bidding the mourners to put their bridal rosemary around the corpse, dress her in the robes in which her wedding was to be celebrated, and carry her to the church. Juliet indeed seems to have married Death. Capulet adds his directions: Everything that was to be used for the wedding festival now will be used for the funeral. The wedding dinner will be a burial feast, the hymns will be dirges, "And all things change them to the contrary." The Friar tells them all to prepare to accompany Juliet's body to the grave, adding this warning: Heaven has punished them for something, and they must now stop all disobedience to heaven's will. All leave, except the Nurse, to do the Friar's bidding.

COMMENT

The calm manner of the Friar as he breaks in on the chorus of grief reminds us of the ironic fact that Juliet is not dead, and that these people grieve for nothing. His consoling words of religious philosophy depict death as a blessing that frees the soul to eternal life. The Friar's comment that the best marriage is that of a girl who dies young is surely descriptive of the marriage of Romeo and Juliet. Their love is such that we cannot picture them having children and growing old together. It is too ecstatic and swift a passion for that, and it moves by its own power toward some earlier end. The image of Juliet as married to Death, begun earlier in the scene by Lord Capulet, is picked up by the Friar. The tone is changed from bitterness to celebration—of Juliet's gaining a place in heaven by becoming Death's bride. As if to emphasize this, she will be mourned and buried in her bridal clothes. We remember how she took the potion in an effort to join her husband and complete her marriage in death. Capulet still feels this reversal, this "contrary" as being cruel, but he concedes. All contraries—death and marriage, love and hate—seem to be growing together.

As the mourners go to church, the musicians remain behind, preparing to leave also. Most likely they are the same musicians who played at Capulet's party, when Paris was to consider his proposed bride, and when Romeo and Juliet fell in love. The Nurse tells them to pack up their instruments, commenting how pitiful is the state of things, and goes herself to mourn. Peter, one of Capulet's servants, comes in. He asks for the song "Heart's ease" to ease his heart, for, he says, his heart itself is playing the tune "My heart is full of woe." Peter is sad, but it is the musicians who feel that music would be inappropriate. Yet gaiety gets the better of them, and instead of making music, they exchange witticisms about music and the money they hope to earn by it. Finally, they go off, planning to wait until the mourners return, so that they may have a free dinner.

COMMENT

This scene is short and light-hearted, giving comic relief—that is, a chance to rest from sorrow and laugh a bit—to the audience. We do not feel that the scoffers are profane, for we know Juliet is not really dead. The real gaiety here mocks the Friar's philosophic happiness; it also mocks the previous scenes when merriment was tinged with irony. We have been given a breather before the long, tragic ascent of the next act.

SUMMARY

This is one of the few scenes in the play devoted to outsiders rather than to the lovers. From one point of view, it shows how the adult world reacts to grief: not individually, nor with any particular distinction of will and imagination, but in a collective chorus of sorrow. At the same time, the theme of love in death and marriage to death, which relates directly to the lovers, is explored. In this way the lovers, their predicament, and their images are kept uppermost in our minds.

This act has been a short one, and full of interludes. It has increased our sense of impending doom by concentrating on the proposed marriage of Paris to Juliet and by the ruse to avoid this marriage, which involves a temporary death on Juliet's part. The death-sleep gives full play to imaginings of the horror of the grave and to the grief of the family. The speed of the action has been increased by the ironic interludes, by moving up the day of the wedding, and by strengthening our own feeling that all speed is necessary to escape the threat that hangs over the lovers. By now, the play is moving at a reckless pace.

ROMEO AND JULIET
ACT V

ACT V, SCENE 1

The scene is Mantua, where Romeo is in exile. Surprisingly, he is in a light-hearted, elevated frame of mind. If he may trust the flattery of dreams, joyful news must be coming to him. He relates his dream: "I dreamt my lady came and found me dead." Juliet came to him and revived him by breathing kisses of life on his lips; and when he regained life, he found he was an emperor. Romeo sighs happily, reflecting that love is so sweet that even its shadows and sorrows, such as this separation from Juliet, are "rich in joy."

COMMENT

To Romeo, the important part of the dream is that he saw Juliet. She came to him and kissed him, bringing life with her. Perhaps he does feel dead without her; at any rate, he is so in love that the mere appearance of his bride seems a good omen, and he is not struck by the part of the dream that immediately catches our attention: Romeo as dead. Forebodings of some misfortune have piled up gradually as the play progressed, and after the last scene, we are alert to references to death. The entire last act has dealt with Juliet since Romeo's absence. Vivid in our minds is the scene when she takes the potion and goes, as she imagines, to join Romeo in death. That Romeo should respond to such a dark dream with such joy seems like the last possible irony.

At this point, the messenger, whom Romeo's dream has led him to expect with happiness, appears. It is Balthasar, a servant of the Montague household, come fresh from Verona. Romeo welcomes him heartily, showering him with questions: Is there a letter from the Friar? How is Juliet? And his parents? Before Balthasar can answer any of these, Romeo asks again about Juliet, "For nothing can be ill if she be well." In that case, nothing goes ill, answers Balthasar, but he speaks more slowly, and with a marked difference of tone. Juliet is well, for her body is in the tomb and her soul is with the angels. The servant watched her being placed in the Capulet vault and then hurried to Mantua to tell Romeo. At this point, Balthasar breaks his somber tone and begs Romeo's pardon for bringing him such news. Romeo's first words come slowly. He is stricken and almost unbelieving as he says, "Is it even so?" And then, in a burst, in one short, ringing phrase, he expresses his reaction: "Then I defy you, stars!"

COMMENT

Balthasar brings the news as he knows it, and he is very sorry that he must tell his master this. He delivers the information without beating around the bush, but at the same time philosophically, for he is trying to offer Romeo the same kind of religious consolation that the Friar offered Juliet's parents—that Juliet is well off, because she is in heaven. It is Romeo's response to which we pay attention. We hear none of the grief-stricken wailing, no berating of the untimeliness of death, none of the chorus of woe, that we heard when Juliet was discovered in deathlike sleep on her bed. Romeo's mourning is one line long, for from here on his life and actions will be his mourning. It is not only distinctly individual, this line of his; it is marked with a range of emotion, poetry, and strength that cannot be found in all the many lines with which Juliet has been mourned in the preceding scene. Romeo is bewildered and hurt beyond belief by the immensity of this loss; his mind cannot encompass the misery that has struck so swiftly, and he questions that it can be true. Then, summoning himself, he defies the stars in heaven. The stars, shining in the dark of night, have watched over the love he shared with Juliet. When he first saw her on the balcony, her eyes seemed like the stars. As night, when the stars shine, has been the only time their love was blessed; the stars have always seemed beneficent. Yet, there is a second meaning for stars. They are the directors of fate and fortune, and they influence the actions of human beings. From the Prologue on, the lovers have been "star-crossed," or ill-fated. In defying the stars, Romeo expresses his feeling of having been betrayed. The stars seemed to bless him in love but now show themselves treacherous. Fortune and fate have turned against him and have done their worst in killing the one thing he treasured. He will defy fate now, not be governed by it. He will act in spite of it, taking his life in his own hands.

Immediately, with headlong speed, Romeo begins to act. He asks Balthasar to go to the place where Romeo has been staying, get a pen and paper, and hire horses; for Romeo intends to leave tonight. The good servant, seeing his master looking "pale and wild," fears that Romeo is about to do something rash and cautions patience. Romeo protests that Balthasar is mistaken and should hurry away on these errands. Almost as an afterthought, he asks whether there are no letters for him from the Friar. When the servant assures him that there are none, Romeo shrugs and hastens him on, promising to join Balthasar soon.

COMMENT

We do not know Romeo's intention, but we are as sure as Balthasar that it is an impetuous one. That Balthasar suggests caution makes clear once again how far removed from the world's understanding Romeo has become. He lives alone in a world of love, distant from all things mundane and moderate, and now that Juliet is gone he is truly isolated. The strength of character he has gained through loving shows in the simplicity with which Romeo grieves, in his defiance and his immediate action. He feels he has no time but must rush to

Verona and Juliet. The scene is imbued with a sense of overwhelming haste, with only a single pause: Romeo's question about a letter from Friar Laurence. We wonder, ourselves, remembering that such a letter was to have been sent, and that had it arrived, Romeo would now know that his Juliet is alive.

Romeo's intention is promptly clarified. His first words after Balthasar's departure are "Well, Juliet, I will lie with thee to-night." Without wasting a second, he begins to consider how he will carry out his intention. Romeo quickly remembers an apothecary (a druggist) situated not far from where he is now. The man was obviously poor: dressed in rags, thin, miserable, and worried. His shop had looked shabby, its shelves bare except for what trifles he had managed to put on them for the sake of appearances. As Romeo had passed by, the pathetic poverty had caught his eye, and the thought had come to him that only from such a person could one buy poison. (The penalty for selling poison in Mantua was death, and only someone desperately in need of money would take the risk.) Romeo finds the shop and calls the apothecary to him.

COMMENT

Romeo's first line deserves attention. His intent in all these hurried actions becomes frighteningly clear. He will go to Juliet's tomb, enter it, and there he will take his own life. He will die at the side of his dead beloved, and in death he will join her. The word "lie" brings in a symbolic meaning as well. To lie with someone is to have sexual intercourse, an act often referred to in literature as "dying." Here, the sexual act, which consummates the marriage of two bodies, has come to mean the same as death, which completes the marriage of two souls in eternal life. Death and marriage are one, and Romeo is going to his death and eternal marriage with Juliet. It is appropriate that Romeo's mind lights on poison as the means to this eternal end. Poison has figured in the play since the Friar mentioned his knowledge of such lore in his first speech. Juliet has taken a similar drug, which has brought her so close to death that everyone, Romeo included, believes her dead. Before taking the potion, the horrors of death loomed large in her mind. Indeed, she reacted to it as though it were poison. In taking it at last, her mind was so confused with death that she thought Romeo was dead, and she was going to join him in death, the eternal marriage, just as he now proposes to join her. The entire scene of her mourning parents equated death and marriage; it prepared us for this one. That equation is now fully realized, and the theme of death as the consummation of love becomes the motivating force of the action.

Romeo now talks to the apothecary, offering him forty ducats (a large sum of money, as ducats were made of gold) in exchange for a dram of the quickest-acting, most fatal poison he can provide. Romeo describes graphically the effects he wishes this poison to have. The apothecary admits that he has "such mortal drugs" but adds that the penalty for selling them is death. "Art thou so bare, and full of wretchness,/ And fear'est to die?" Romeo points out that starvation, oppression, and contempt are clearly shown in the apothecary's appearance. Clearly, no one in such an extreme of misery can think that the world and its laws are his friends, or that such laws will make him rich. Break the law, Romeo urges, and by breaking it, get rid of this poverty. The apothecary consents because of his poverty but against his will. The apothecary gives him enough poison to kill twenty people instantly. Romeo pays him, commenting that the gold is a worse poison and kills more people than this liquid does. He says goodbye, adding kindly to this man that he should buy food and get some flesh on him. The poison is, for Romeo, a cordial or sweet liquor to be used at Juliet's grave.

COMMENT

Romeo's character has greatly broadened. Even in the midst of his distress, he has much sympathy for this poor apothecary. Indeed, he helps the apothecary keep his pride by his manner of persuasion, his realization that one's will means more than one's poverty, and his recognition that gold can be an evil drug, although the world and its laws do not recognize this. He seems to sense a kinship with the apothecary, in that they both suffer so much and are so alienated from the world as to risk death. Romeo, who feels so close to death himself, is surprised only that the apothecary hesitates for an instant at the thought of the death penalty.

SUMMARY

Much worth noting has happened in this short scene.

(1) Romeo, hearing of Juliet's death, has chosen to join her. The marriage of death is fast becoming the controlling image of the play.

(2) Romeo has shown the greatness of his character and imagination in his short but profound reaction to the tragic news.

(3) The impetuous speed that has been characteristic of the love now becomes part of Romeo's conscious will, as he hurries to his death.

(4) Fate, which has threatened the lovers throughout the play, now seems to hold full sway. At the same time, Romeo defies fate, taking control of his actions. This double aspect of fate and the defiance of fate seems contradictory. To understand it, one must realize that love has transformed Romeo and Juliet. They have gained their stature as characters through it, and we know them primarily as lovers rather than as people. Each has chosen this love and, in such an impetuously quick, passionate love, a quick and early end is inherent. True

romantic love can have no other alternative. It is like a meteor, a streak of light that fills the sky for a moment and then disappears in darkness forever. As the Friar has said, "These violent delights have violent ends," and it was he who compared such passion to the kiss of fire and powder, the very meeting of which causes the destruction of both. The Friar has also made the statement "She's best married that dies married young," meaning that such love is the highest. In choosing this kind of love, the lovers choose their own end. In that sense, they have a hand in their own fate, just as the seemingly involuntary speed of the play is a result of the love they have chosen and the lovers they have chosen to be. The critics' maxim that character is fate echoes in our minds here, as Romeo bends his will toward accomplishing the death that fate has decreed, becoming both the master of and mastered by that fate.

ACT V, SCENE 2

Once again we find ourselves in Verona, and at the cell of Friar Laurence. Someone is knocking and calling at his door, and the Friar answers eagerly. Upon conceiving the desperate plan to help Juliet and giving her the potion, he had sent, as promised, a message to Romeo in Mantua explaining the plan. Two days have passed, and he expects that his messenger, a monk named Friar John, will be returning now with Romeo's reply. It is indeed Friar John at the door, and Friar Laurence welcomes him, pressing him for Romeo's answer. But Friar John has another story to tell, and one that bodes no good. He had gone to find yet another monk to accompany him to Mantua. This third friar had been visiting the sick, and as Friar John spoke to him of the journey, searchers came. The job of searchers was to roam through Verona and seal up houses where people with infectious diseases lived, thus preventing such sickness from spreading. These searchers sealed up the house where Friar John and his companion were talking, suspecting it to be some such house of disease. Friar John could not get out; he never reached Mantua. Fearfully, Friar

Laurence asks who did take the letter to Romeo. The sad answer is that no one did. People were so afraid of catching the disease that Friar John could persuade no one to take the letter to Mantua, nor even to return it to Friar Laurence.

COMMENT

This answers our question, and Romeo's, as to why he has not heard from Friar Laurence. Chance and accident once again have joined with fate, and the result is another grave, unforseeable misfortune for the lovers. We know that if Romeo had received the Friar's letter, he would not now be in his present desperate and final state of mind.

Shocked, Friar Laurence cries out, "Unhappy fortune." He explains that the letter was not trivial but concerned directions of great importance. He asks Friar John to help him now by finding an iron crowbar and bringing it to the cell quickly. Friar John, seeing he has inadvertently had part in causing some calamity, is all too willing to be of help; he leaves immediately. Friar Laurence then expresses his own intention to go to Juliet's vault alone. She will be awakening within three hours, and he is sure that she will blame him severely for not having notified Romeo. The Friar's plan is to take the young girl from her tomb and hide her in his cell while he sends yet another message to Romeo, telling him to come for his wife. Feeling very sorry for Juliet, who is "closed in a dead man's tomb," the Friar leaves.

COMMENT

What the Friar does not know is that Romeo has heard of Juliet's supposed death—and that he is coming to join her in death. The failure of his message to reach Romeo is far more fatefully serious than the Friar imagines. We know the good Friar will do his best, but the blunders of accident and the swiftness of fate seem to be more than he will be able to handle. Still, there is some hope that he will reach the vault in time, meet Romeo there, and be able to block the course the action has taken. This scene makes it clear that the speed of what is happening forms the greatest threat and that only perfect timing will prevent tragedy. Speed and timing, which grew out of the impetuous love, have become movers of action.

ACT V, SCENE 3

We come now, at night, to the place on which all the action converges. It is a graveyard and the vault of the Capulet household. We expect various people, but the visitor we see there now was not expected. It is Paris, come with flowers to the tomb of the girl he loved and intended to marry. He has a young boy with him, a page who carries his torch. Paris tells the boy to put out the torch, so that they will not be discovered. The boy is to lie down under the nearby yew trees and to put his ear to the ground. As the earth of the churchyard is loose from the constant digging of graves, the boy will be able to hear the approach of any footsteps, and can whistle a warning to Paris. The page is a bit afraid, all alone in a graveyard, but he goes off to obey his master. Turning to face the closed vault where Juliet lies, Paris mourns, "Sweet flower, with flowers thy bridal bed I strew."

The bridal bed is made of dusty stone, for it is a tomb, and Paris intends to come each night to water it with his tears and strew it with flowers, as he does now. When the page's whistle pierces the air, Paris wonders "what cursed foot" has come to interrupt this ritual of love's grief. Seeing a torch, he begs the night to hide him from view and withdraws a bit from the site.

COMMENT

Paris grieves sincerely. He has never done anything to make us dislike him, and that he loved Juliet truly we do not doubt. His images in grief are those with which she was first mourned—as a girl in the flower of life who was to be his bride but who has become death's bride instead. Paris is not original, but he is genuine. The yew trees mentioned are symbols of sorrow. The night, always so welcomed by the lovers, is feared by Paris's page. Indeed, we are struck by the fact that if Paris's grief and love were equal in force to Romeo's, he would not be content to mourn. The contrast between the two is made clear.

It is Romeo who approaches. He is just arrived from Mantua, and with him is his servant, Balthasar, who carries a torch, a hammer, and a crowbar. Romeo, unaware that he is being watched, takes the tools and torch from Balthasar and gives him a letter. The letter is to Romeo's father, and Balthasar is to deliver it early the next morning. Romeo instructs the faithful servant not to try and restrain him. He explains that he is going to "descend into this bed of death"—that is, enter the tomb—partly to see his lady's face, but mostly in order to take from her finger a precious and important ring. Balthasar must leave immediately; if he is suspicious and returns, Romeo threatens to tear him limb from limb and cast his remains all over the churchyard: "The time and my intents are savage-wild,/ More fierce and more inexorable far/ Than empty tigers or the roaring sea." When Balthasar promises to leave his master alone, Romeo assures him that only by doing so can Balthasar show his friendship. Romeo gives the servant money and wishes him well in life. Despite all this, Balthasar mutters to himself as he leaves that since he fears his master's looks and doubts his intentions, he will hide nearby.

COMMENT

That Romeo is highly wrought up is clear from his manner of speaking. His phrases are short and jerky, abrupt and to the point. His tone to the servant is harshly commanding. His threat to Balthasar is not a pretty one; he seems to compare himself to a savage beast. We know very well that he has a desperate plan in mind and that he is not going into Juliet's tomb for any ring. It can be easily surmised that the letter to his father will explain his suicide. Balthasar himself senses from his master's wildness of manner that something is afoot; and despite the threats, the servant feels his presence may be of some value.

Romeo picks up once more the imagery of death and marriage by calling Juliet's tomb a "bed of death." Visually, the sight of the impassioned young man holding the torch aloft in the darkness would recall to the audience the imagery of his love as a light at night, a brilliance in the darkness. His intention is clear, but he says that the time, as well as the intent, is fierce and inexorable. He has already taken hold of his destiny. By now his love and the very speed of this action he has determined on have him in grip. There is no going back; his death-marriage he has chosen, and it is not to be avoided now, for the time is at hand and has control. It is a complex relation between his own free choice and unavoidable fate that Romeo expresses in this one sentence.

Romeo approaches the tomb he is about to open. He addresses it, calling it a "Womb of death" and an awful mouth that has filled itself with Juliet, "the dearest morsel of the earth." With his tools, he pries open the "rotten jaws"—that is, the door of the vault—declaring that to spite this mouth of death for taking Juliet, he will cram it with more food—his own dead body.

COMMENT

Romeo is involved in a fierce action. His language is vivid with the hate he feels at death for taking Juliet and with the abandon in which he will get his revenge on death by killing himself, thus reaching Juliet anyway. The speech is a single rich, developed metaphor; again the theme of the sexual consummation of marriage in death is struck by the words "Womb of death," addressed by Romeo to his beloved's tomb. To enter such a "womb" is to begin the final sexual act, which will climax in dying. The mouth that has swallowed Juliet is the mouth of the womb of death.

Paris has been watching all this, infuriated by what he sees. As he understands it, Romeo has murdered Juliet's cousin; and since it is believed that Juliet died of her grief over Tybalt's death, Romeo is indirectly her murderer. Now the banished Montague has the nerve to come and threaten to shame the bodies he has killed. Paris emerges from his hiding and shouts at Romeo, commanding him to stop this unholy action. Does Romeo really think he need carry revenge further than death? Paris wants to arrest Romeo and take him to his death sentence for breaking his exile. "Thou must die," cries Paris, to which Romeo replies, "I must indeed; and therefore came I hither." Romeo does not know who cries at him from the darkness. He pleads to the person not to tempt him, for he is desperate and easily urged to a fury that would bring the sin of another killing on his head. Romeo begs Paris to leave, saying, "By heaven, I love thee better than myself,/ For I come hither armed against myself." Paris, however, refuses; he continues to try to arrest Romeo. It is almost with a sigh that Romeo, seeing no other alternative, begins to fight. Seeing them, the page runs to call the guards. Romeo kills Paris, whose dying request is to be laid beside Juliet in the tomb. Hearing the request, Romeo looks at the face of this young man he has killed and recognizes Paris, cousin of his friend Mercutio. Vaguely he remembers that on the swift ride from Mantua, Balthasar told him that Paris was to have married Juliet. Romeo's mind was so distracted during that ride that he is not sure whether he heard this, dreamed it, or just madly assumes it because of Paris's last request. But he will fulfill the request, and he carries dead Paris to "a triumphant grave" in Juliet's tomb.

COMMENT

Paris, of course, knows nothing of what there has been between Romeo and Juliet. He has every reason to suspect the most vile motives on Romeo's part in coming here. Though Paris is not a violent man, he cannot watch to see what will happen; he must attempt an arrest. Romeo's state of mind permits no interruption. Their fight is inevitable.

Paris's death saddens us. Paris has done no wrong. Throughout the play, he has appeared to be honorable and of fine sensibility. His only fault was loving Juliet, and he could not have prevented this. The love was not returned, the marriage never realized; now, in an effort to protect his love, he has been killed, without even knowing the true state of things. We feel he has suffered unduly at the hands of fate.

Romeo speaks from the heart in trying to persuade Paris to leave. He knows too well that the only other alternative is a fight to the death, and he wishes only to kill himself, not this young man. On hearing Paris's last request to be placed near Juliet, Romeo feels immediate kinship for him. It would have been Romeo's own request, had the result of the fight been different. When he realizes that here is another who has loved Juliet and died for her, he sympathizes and determines to do his best for Paris. There is no jealousy here; Romeo's character has widened beyond that.

As he carries Paris into the tomb, Romeo hears himself calling it a grave. It is not a grave, he says, but a lantern, for Juliet's beauty transforms it to a "feasting place full of light." He lays Paris down, commenting that this dead man has now been buried by another dead man and how, before death, men are known to make merry. Such merriment is called the "lightning before death," and he wonders if that is his present state. He sees Juliet fully now and exclaims, "O my love! my wife."

Death has not lessened her beauty; and Romeo, seeing how the color still remains in her face, says, "Thou art not conquer'd; beauty's ensign yet/ Is crimson in thy lips and in thy cheeks,/ And death's pale flag is not advanced there." Seeing Tybalt's sheet-covered corpse, Romeo thinks that by killing himself, he will be killing Tybalt's enemy and murderer and avenging his death. "Forgive me, cousin!" he says, and turns back to Juliet, puzzling that she has remained so beautiful. To his distracted mind, it seems that "unsubstantial Death" is in love with Juliet, and keeps her here in the dark to be its beloved. Romeo can't allow that: He will stay in this "palace of dim night" with Juliet forever, taking his eternal rest, and will "Shake the yoke of inauspicious stars/ From this world-wearied flesh." He takes his last look at his beloved, his last embrace, and with his kiss he seals finally "A dateless bargain with engrossing Death." Drawing the vial of poison from his pocket, he invokes it as the bitter and desperate pilot that will guide the boat of his body, sick and tired of this sea of life, onto the rocks of death. With the gesture of a toast—"Here's to my love!"—Romeo drinks down the poison he calls a cordial. The drug is quick. His lips move from the kiss of the poison to Juliet's lips, and "With a kiss I die."

COMMENT

Romeo says that a dead man brings dead Paris to a tomb. He means himself. With his decision to die, he parted from life. He accepted his fate with such determination to force it to a conclusion that he feels himself to be dead. He has grown to maturity so quickly that he even calls his own contemporary, Paris, "young." Now Romeo waits to join Juliet. When he sees her, his breath is taken by her beauty. He remarks more than once that she seems alive, untouched by the pallor of death. Indeed, the ironically tragic reason for this is that Juliet is alive and on the verge of waking. It is all a matter of timing, but Romeo rushes to his own death. He has bargained with death for Juliet, and all he needs to implement his own death and to join her is a guide—the poison. He dies, as he wished, beside Juliet. His final gesture is a toast, much like Juliet's previous toast to him when she took the potion, and with it, symbolic death.

Romeo's entire speech brings a final resolution to the imagery of light and dark. The lovers always have loved at night, and their love was the source of all light for them. Now, in the darkness of death in a tomb, love sheds enough light to transform the vault into a festival of brilliance. At the same time, the vault is a "palace of dim night." These two contraries are possible now, for marriage has become one with death, so that light and darkness mean the same thing. For the sake of love, Romeo has chosen to submit to darkness, to die, in order to live eternally in the light of love with Juliet. Love is light, death is darkness; and as love and death are inseparable, so are their corresponding images. Their love has been a meteor, a brilliant flash in the night that fades quickly. But as the darkness of death takes over, eternal light is promised. So Romeo shakes off at last the "yoke" that fate has placed on him.

By accepting willfully the death that can't be avoided, that was destined by the very quality of love he shared with Juliet, Romeo in one gesture—his own murder—accepts his fate and transcends it. We grieve, but we sense his triumph. Furthermore, we are aware that the images of light and dark, love and death, the stars and fate, have reached their resolution and climatic conclusion. But Juliet is alive. The failure of timing, which accounts for the Friar's failure to be here by now and Juliet's not waking just moments earlier, will be enough to insure an equally tragic and triumphant death for her.

At this point the Friar, who has hurried so much that he has managed to stumble over every grave in his path, appears. He carries tools for opening the vault but sees, to his surprise, that the Capulet tomb is open and lit from within by a torch. Meeting Balthasar, he asks whose torch it is in the tomb. The servant replies that it is Romeo's and that he has been there a full half an hour. Balthasar has sworn at the threat of death not to stay, so he fears to accompany the Friar and show himself to Romeo. But he does tell the monk that he has had a dream that Romeo fought and killed another man before entering the tomb. The Friar is filled with fear that something has gone amiss. He advances to the tomb, calling Romeo's name, and soon finds bloodstains and swords to witness the truth of Balthasar's dream. In a moment the Friar sees Romeo, all pale, and with him a bloody Paris. No sooner has he taken this in than he sees Juliet stir and waken. She sees the Friar, but she is yet oblivious to the head that lies heavily on her breast. Remembering everything in a flood, she asks, "Where is my Romeo?" Approaching noises are heard, and the Friar urges Juliet quickly to leave this "nest/ Of death, contagion, and unnatural sleep:/ A greater power than we can contradict/ Hath thwarted our intents." He tells her that on her bosom lies her dead husband, that Paris is dead as well, and that he will find a place for her in a convent of nuns. She must come now, without questions, for the guards are coming and the Friar does not dare stay. As Juliet refuses to move, he flees.

COMMENT

The Friar's actions have lately struck us as of dubious wisdom, though we know they are full of good intentions. This scene confirms for us what we sensed in him: a certain lack of moral strength. He is grieved and shocked to the extent that he loses his moderation and fails to comprehend how Juliet must feel. And he is too frightened at the enormity of the tragedy to be able to face his responsibility for Juliet's life now. What frightens him is the thought of the blame that society will put on him if his involvement becomes known. He feels guilty, and he runs. Juliet's answer to the Friar when he begs her to leave is scornful. The child-turned-woman has wakened from death and has found her lover incomprehensibly dead and her comforter, the Friar, ready to flee in fear of discovery. It is too much.

Juliet is left alone, to do what she must. Her mind is clear about her love for Romeo, so much so that she scarcely has time to express it or her overpowering grief at his death before she goes to join him. She sees a cup in his hand and realizes that he has poisoned himself only moments too soon. She chides him, in her gentle way, at having left no poison for her. She feels so close to him and to death that she can scold sweetly for a moment before she kisses his lips to see if any poison is left there. Having kissed Romeo she murmurs, "Thy lips are warm," and the pathos of that cry brings down on us like a bludgeon how this accelerated action has doomed the love, how the lovers' happiness hung on a few fateful minutes. It was lost because Juliet had not quite awakened and Romeo had not been able to waste a moment in joining her. Juliet now hears the voices of the guards; she, too, senses the need for speed. She takes Romeo's dagger and stabs herself, saying, "This is thy sheath; there rust, and let me die."

COMMENT

Juliet, like Romeo, loves faithfully beyond death and goes willingly to join her lover in death and eternity, the final marriage. There is almost nothing to say at this point in the play. Romeo and Juliet have died tragically. The ironies of fate and timing have run their course and can do no more. We are stricken with a sense of the beauty of this love—and with the tragic inevitability with which it led the lovers to an early end. Yet we know that such love had to end soon and sadly, and we realize that the beauty of it has justified the grief we feel now. The death-marriage is a triumph.

The guards, led by Paris's page, enter abruptly. Seeing blood, some leave to search the grounds. It is clear that Juliet is newly dead. Messengers are sent to Prince Escalus, the Capulets, and the Montagues, and the guards are puzzled. They cannot comprehend from this slaughter what has happened. Balthasar and the Friar have been found; they are brought in and held for questioning. Now the Prince enters, with Lord and Lady Capulet close behind him. All have heard cries of fear in the streets, and now the guard tells them of the three deaths. Balthasar and the Friar are being brought forward for questioning, but this is interrupted by the Capulets, both of them overcome with horror at the sight of Juliet's fresh blood and the Montague dagger "mis-sheathed" in her breast. Lord Montague enters on this cue. His wife has died, during the night, of grief at her son's exile. What other grief awaits him? With something akin to resignation, Montague sees his son and heir, dead before his time. The Prince now calls a halt to all mourning, in order that the ambiguities and complications of this triple death may be clarified. He calls the suspects, and the Friar steps forward "both to impeach and purge" himself of all this murder. As quickly and simply as he can, he tells the story of the love and marriage of Romeo and Juliet, Tybalt's death, Romeo's exile, the betrothal of Juliet to Paris, his own plan to save her from dishonor, the accident of the letter failing to reach its destination, and the inevitable end. The Nurse will bear witness to the marriage, says the Friar, adding that, if it is judged that any of this is his fault, he will accept the death penalty. Prince Escalus pardons him. Balthasar now speaks, and gives to the Prince the letter Romeo had meant for his father. The letter supports the Friar's statement, and the story has been put back together.

COMMENT

The scene is long and stern. It shows the grief of the Prince and the two households, and it gives the Friar a chance to stand for himself. His tale emphasizes the faults of fate, of haste, and of the feuding families as well as his own, and we see that he deserves our pardon as well as the Prince's. It prepares us for the final judgment.

Calling the two feuding families to him, the Prince admonishes, "See what a scourge is laid upon your hate,/ That heaven finds means to kill your joys with love." The Prince himself has lost two relatives by not punishing the feuders harshly enough to make them stop. Capulet and Montague, each pledging gold statues of the other's child, shake hands and vow to feud no more. The play ends on a note of "glooming peace," for "The sun for sorrow will not raise his head." The Prince challenges everyone to think this over, and closes the play with this comment: "Never was a story of more woe,/ Than this of Juliet and her Romeo."

COMMENT

The play has come full circle, completing itself as was foretold in the Prologue. All true poetry has fled with the lives of the lovers, and the ending seems grey. The stars have led here, and the final irony of fate lies in the sacrifice of the joys of the parents in order to cure their mutual hate and in the fact that the sacrifice was made through love. From the outside point of view (perhaps fate's view), this reconciliation of the feud was the point of the play. To us, the play has been about Romeo, Juliet, and the beauty of their tragic love.

The play started with a street fight between the houses, at which the Prince appeared and which he censured heavily. The tragic turning was Mercutio's death, and Prince Escalus was present then, to punish and warn further. Now, this figure of justice, judgment, and peace presides over the final scene, clinches the reconciliation, mourns the lovers, and gives us our sense of the completed structure of the play as it ends.

SUMMARY

Every theme of the play has reached its climax and resolved itself. The tragedy has found its mark, and with it, the play's meaning has reached its culmination. To summarize the final scene is to summarize the play, for here flower the seeds planted throughout. Some are as follows:

(1) The contrasting imagery of light and dark has come together, as have the parallel themes of love and death. Light and dark become love and death, and all contraries become inextricably one.

(2) In opposition to these image-clusters has been the outside world: the moderation of age and the hate of the feud. These forces alienated the lovers and their love, and now by their death the same forces are reconciled to peace.

(3) The speed of the fate that has had control throughout is a speed born in the love of Romeo and Juliet. As it grew from the love, so it takes over and leads to death.

The play abounds in the lyricism of love, despite its desperate ending in death. It is world-famous for its portrayal of idealistic young love, faithful till death. As such, many critics consider the play to be not a tragedy of love, but a hymn of praise to this transforming, romantic love that triumphs even over death. The name "Romeo" means "lover" all over the world, for the lovers and their passion have become prototypes. Tragedy has been made beautiful by Shakespeare; and through his art, the theater has become a vehicle for poetry as much as for drama. He achieves this by a formal, almost musical series of contrasts between youth and age, fate and free will, joy and hatred, love and death. During the course of the action, these seemingly incompatible elements grow together like themes in music until they fuse into a single melody.

CHARACTER ANALYSES

ROMEO

During the course of the play, Romeo matures to adulthood. When we first meet him he is a stereotype of the lover—cherishing solitude and night, pensive, pale, and sad. He assumes all the attitudes of a rejected suitor; he writes poetry; his speech is a series of contradictory exclamations. At this juncture, Romeo knows no more about love than what he has read in the books he emulates, and he is actually in love with love. His posturing makes him the brunt of much joking from his worldly, witty friends, Mercutio and Benvolio. They have loved Romeo for his own devil-may-care brilliance, and they sense that his present sadness is not true to him. Their judgment is correct, for all Romeo's mooning about ceases when he meets Juliet; and in loving her he discovers that joy, not sadness, is part of love. After arranging for his marriage to Juliet, Romeo meets Mercutio and Benvolio. His wit is all air and fire, and he parries each of Mercutio's verbal thrusts so brightly that Mercutio is wholly charmed and welcomes back the true Romeo.

But the true Romeo has not yet fully emerged. He is not only a courtly, carefree young man. He is capable of the deepest passions of love. In his initial courtship of Juliet, at her father's party and in the orchard, Romeo's entrancement is still, though feelingly, expressed in somewhat typical gestures of holy adoration. His comparison of Juliet to the source of all light is not wholly new either. Romeo is not an original lover; he is the epitome of all romantic lovers, the consummate lover. In the love duets, the heights of his imagination and expression are equalled by Juliet. It is the thoroughness of his loving, his complete lack of conflict or hesitation in any matter that concerns Juliet, the utter commitment with which he abandons himself to the intense, swift passion, that distinguishes him as a lover. Romeo is not practical or realistic, but his preoccupation is not necessarily indicative of dreamy absentmindedness. When Tybalt is insulting him and goading him to enter combat, neither lack of courage nor lovesickness constrains Romeo. Rather, he is elevated by love for Juliet to an encompassing love that does not permit of fighting, and he is all too conscious of his new status as a relative of his challenger. This complex and moral awareness puts dueling out of the question, but the secrecy of the marriage makes an explanation equally impossible. Romeo's ambiguous retorts are mistaken for softness by his comrades. What really precipitates the fight, then, is the fact that love has completely alienated Romeo from the world. When real honor demands that the youth fight he does so, and revenges Mercutio's death to his own severe detriment. Later, this alienation and consequent lack of practicality emerges more clearly, when Romeo falls to the floor of the Friar's cell in a faint of despair. This does, at first, seem like weakness. Yet the desperate fight, Romeo's exile, his overwhelming love for Juliet, and the total lack of understanding displayed by even the Friar for the all-consuming nature of Romeo's passion provide sufficient explanation for the lapse.

Romeo's ability to die for love comes as no surprise. We are prepared for it by his falling in the Friar's cell and by his willingness, after the wedding night, to risk his life to stay in Verona if Juliet so wishes. It is the manner of Romeo's choosing to die that comes as a revelation. Gone are all traces of the standard responses of a lover. Gone, also, is the momentary inability to act that we noticed in his behavior at the Friar's. With his "I defy you, stars," Romeo takes fate firmly in his hands and determines the time and manner of his own death. In the very brevity of his words and speed of his actions lies Romeo's stature as a character. He does not pause, either for self-indulgent emotion or in lack of conviction, but with unwavering courage he goes to search out his love in death. Love has become life for him, and without Juliet there can be nothing but death in living. Romeo has grown up, but his whole identity as a human being lies in loving. He is not only alienated from the world; he now cares nothing for it or its trappings. He is purely and voluntarily a lover.

Romeo's battle with Paris only demonstrates how much he has forsaken the world. By the time he reaches the tomb he is so given over to death and love, so separate from life and the world, that he can call himself a dead man. His passion now absorbs itself in dying, as it did before in loving. His farewells to life are scarcely farewells. They seem more like greetings to death and Juliet. His imagination and passion have reached their ultimate peak when he dies. In that sense, Romeo has truly triumphed.

JULIET

In the four-day space of the play, Juliet grows from a charming fourteen-year-old child to a woman. Her first appearance with her Nurse and mother as they prepare for the party catches the sweet affirmative aspect of her nature, but she seems merely a docile, untried girl. The Nurse's warm, rambling speech about Juliet's babyhood, with its savoring of the bawdy, gives us a hint of the atmosphere in which this girl grew. Lady Capulet's more cool, sophisticated, and premeditated point of view gives us another. But neither proves to have had much influence, and Juliet seems quite blank until she loves Romeo. The holy aura that surrounds their first meeting aptly emphasizes the girl's innocence. Yet it is she that breaks the mood and shows her true responses when, half blushing at the passion she has aroused, half teasing to cover her emotion, she remarks, "You kiss by the book." Later, in the orchard, it is again Juliet who puts their love on frank and open ground by unwittingly professing her feelings aloud before the hidden lover. These traits of innocent coyness, teasing, and yet openness remain with Juliet throughout. Her gentle images at this meeting are quite her own; for example, her wish that Romeo were her pet bird, whom she would allow to hop away, but who could never escape altogether because of the string she would hold. Juliet enjoys the strain of loving completely, wishes for a longer courtship, and is aware that the sadness of parting is a sweet one. Her perception is expanding rapidly, and she is the practical one who proposes the immediate marriage.

In fact, Juliet is always the practical one, the one who implements action. At the same time, her impatience contributes largely to the speed of the love affair. Waiting for her Nurse to come with news of the marriage plans, waiting for the wedding night to fall, Juliet's passion is clear, as is the vulnerability of the passion. It is at these instances that her imagination becomes extravagant and reaches peaks of exhilaration that result in such poetry as her invocation to the night. She gradually emerges as a girl of much fire as well as charm. But the vulnerability is still there, and the Nurse takes advantage of it in the scene where she tells Juliet of Tybalt's death and Romeo's banishment.

As Juliet grows, she acquires facility with deception. She successfully dupes both her Nurse and her parents concerning her change of heart about marrying Paris. In fact, with her characteristic fervor she succeeds too well, with the result that the marriage is moved forward another day, and the whole pace of the action is quickened. But Juliet's fervor extends as well into her desperation to preserve her honor, and by that she acquires a sternness of will that allows her to affirm the Friar's plan. Her deepening maturity is proved in this, and in her ultimate suicide. At the Friar's before determining on the plan, and again alone in her room when she is about to take the potion, Juliet's fertile imagination runs rampant with visions of the horrors of the grave. But the all-pervasive, all-enveloping nature of this blossoming woman's passion lifts her finally beyond this. When Juliet takes the potion, she does so for the sake of love. She believes she is marrying death in order to join Romeo, whom she envisions dead, and she toasts him triumphantly with the liquid, just as he later toasts her with the poison. To her, as to Romeo, life is where love is. She, like him, is alienated from the world. Finding comfort nowhere, she must rely wholly on herself. Even her scorn for the Friar's fearful flight from the tomb is but a faint emotion. She can scold Romeo in the old, loving way for leaving her no poison. It is with joy that she gives Romeo's dagger its final sheath in her bosom and goes to find love in death, since there is none in this world.

MERCUTIO

The worldly, witty, man-about-town who is Romeo's best friend attracts much attention from the critics. In a sense, Mercutio is one of Shakespeare's dramatic devices. The character wins our liking and is then sacrificed, thus becoming the pivot on which romance turns to tragedy. It is the Queen Mab speech, so often called an irrelevant tangent, that secures our affections for Mercutio. Before that, we are merely charmed by his sophisticated, irreverent, and often bawdy jesting, by his worldly flippancy and cynicism. But the Queen Mab speech transforms him before our eyes. The depth of Mercutio's love for Romeo is evident in this attempt to cheer him. The rare, extravagant fantasy of his vision confronts us, and we truly admire this light-tongued aristocrat. That Mercutio has plumbed deeply human troubles becomes evident in the change of his tone to encompass such images as that of a soldier starting awake from dreams of a bloody battle. Our feelings are truly clinched when Mercutio proceeds to brush off the genius of this speech as a "vain fantasy" which has no real substance. We realize then that Mercutio's scorn emerges from his disillusionment with himself, his sense that his life and being are based on emptiness.

This is not to say that Mercutio dislikes life. He lives with gusto, and he has a strong creed about how to live. The creed is never stated, but it becomes clear to us through negatives, such as Mercutio's intense dislike of Tybalt, whom he refers to derogatorily as the prince of cats. Although Tybalt is an able fighter, he is also, in Mercutio's eyes, a shallow dandy with ridiculous affectations, lacking in any true manliness. For this, Mercutio detests him. When Tybalt begins his sally at Romeo, and Romeo does not respond, Mercutio must. Not only is he ashamed at Romeo's weakness and lack of sense of honor, he is enraged by Tybalt's sassiness. When Tybalt strikes home because of Romeo's attempt to keep peace, it is too much. Mercutio is dying, but he utters a stream of invective against the senseless feud and against Tybalt, the creature who lives by narrow rules and scratches the life out of others. Mercutio always has taken pride in his own realism. Now he has taken up his sword to fend off infamy from his true ideals of manhood and selfhood. For those ideals he dies, but not easily. He goes down vehemently, giving vent to bitterness and cynicism with all the wry wit for which we know him.

THE NURSE

Here we have one of the simplest, yet most fully alive, characters in the play. The Nurse delights and dismays us often, at times even simultaneously. She is an old woman whose thoughts reveal a genuine relish for all things concerning sex, especially the simplest and lowest forms of bawdry. Her vivid, colloquial speech follows the ramblings of her mind, resulting in repetitions and irrelevancies, such as we see in her ribald account of Juliet as a child. She enjoys anything glamorous and is pleased to take the airs of a lady when bearing messages between her mistress and Romeo. She assumes this role with aplomb, and she is as much herself in such a ridiculous posture as when she drops the role for a round of curses at the disappearing Mercutio, who has made fun of her.

The Nurse has many privileges at the Capulets'; she can talk back to the Lord when he is in ill temper and tease him when he feels cheerful. She takes her liberties too far with Juliet, however. For the Nurse indulges herself fully in whatever twinges of emotion she can, and such self-indulgence can become cruelty. Taking advantage of her age, and wishing for a little sympathy from Juliet, she treats the fervent, impatient girl to an agonizingly long digression before she will tell her the wedding plans. More cruel and offensive still is the Nurse's presentation of the news that Tybalt is dead and Romeo sentenced to exile. The Nurse's rambling and exclaiming is, in this case, deliberately contrived to squeeze the last drop of emotion from the situation. She is indulging her taste for excesses of passion, if vicariously, and Juliet suffers by it.

Thus, the Nurse's predilection for the lower passions makes it impossible for her to understand Juliet. One could have expected their final alienation. The Nurse's suggestion that Juliet abandon Romeo and marry Paris is, for Juliet, the final blow. But this response to the situation is exactly what we look for from the Nurse. It is hardy, callous realism, based on her intrinsic belief that life is to be enjoyed, no matter how. Nothing less than the death of Juliet, whom she really did love, can reduce this garrulous Nurse to a creature pained beyond her powers of expression. For that is how we see her last.

FRIAR LAURENCE

The gentle Friar plays a linking role in the play, for he is the only true connection between the lovers, with their isolated passion, and the harsh outside world. A sympathetic person, he uses all the means at his disposal to make the love possible and at the same time to reconcile it with the exigencies of reality. He first condones the love as a means for bringing an end to the bitter feud. To this end, and simultaneously to promote the happiness of the two young people, he performs the marriage. When the complications of Romeo's exile and Juliet's proposed marriage to Paris ensue, he uses his knowledge of herbs to effect the best solution he can and does his best to inform Romeo. That the message never reaches its destination is not the Friar's fault.

This linking role, coupled with the philosophy he expounds, shows the Friar as a creature of reason. Often he counsels Romeo to be more temperate, and he does this with the young man's happiness at heart. He hopes to save the lovers from the violent end to which such violent passions often lead. But precisely because of this belief in moderation and reason, the Friar fails to understand the lovers. To him, the degree to which their love is absolute, and the beauty and speed that consequently is engendered, are all inconceivable.

But this failure of understanding is not his alone; it is true of all the characters in the play, with the difference that only the Friar tries to understand. What we do consider a fault is his failure in moral strength. The Friar lectured Romeo severely for losing control of himself when faced with exile. Again, it was he that brought the wailing grief over Juliet to an end, directing the participants to take control of themselves, find solace in religion, and begin the necessary preparations for the funeral. The Friar has stood for moral strength, but when, in the tomb, he is faced with the freshly dead bodies of Paris and Romeo, and the intractability of Juliet, the Friar cannot face the responsibility of his own role in all this. In the end, it is society he sides with, for it is the censure of society he fears when he runs guiltily away. In presenting his defense, he seems forgivable, but his stature has diminished in our eyes. We see him at last as a well-intentioned pawn in a game played between fate and the passion of love. It is merely regrettable that this gentle, reasonable man has not the height or breadth of feeling to comprehend either one of the two.

LORD CAPULET

This touchy, talkative aristocrat has but one position in life: master of his household. To lose this command would be to lessen his own imposing stature. When it suits him, Capulet is expansive, generous, and hearty. He can leave the decision about her marriage to his daughter; he can warmly welcome masked intruders at his party, even if they come from the enemy household. But where it concerns the public image of his own house, Lord Capulet's will is inviolate. He forbids Tybalt to disrupt his party with a fight, and for all his genial mood, his temper bristles at Tybalt's slightest indication of going against his wishes. When further fighting clouds the Capulet name, the Lord becomes politic. He would not lose favor with Verona's Prince, so he makes final the arrangements for his daughter to marry Paris, a relative of the Prince. He retracts his more generous offer to let Juliet decide for herself and decides for her. He actually cannot conceive that she would oppose his wishes, and it comes as a shock when she does. To be balked like this, to have his will crossed, seems to him like outright denial of his position as lord of the house. Capulet becomes enraged. His language throughout is colorful, but in this state of infuriation, it becomes scathing. He streams forth a series of vilifying rebukes at his daughter, calling her to task for her impudence and threatening to turn her out on the street if she does not suit her will to his.

But Capulet, for all his willfulness and ill temper, is a creature of feeling. He genuinely loves his daughter and overindulges himself in his extreme rage. He is gentle with her again before she even apologizes, and his delight with her pretended change of heart is pathetic, in view of the circumstances. Nothing will do for her then but a great festivity, and he happily gives up a night's sleep to arrange it. All his genial, free speech flows back, and he jests merrily. When Juliet is discovered dead, this man of abundant, rich language is at first struck silent. When he does speak, the tenderness with which he images his grief sets the tone for the chorus of mourning. His role in the play is as a partisan of hatred, but Shakespeare has made him into a solid character, comparable to the old Nurse in the simple completeness of his being.

CRITICISM

THE CRITICS ON ROMEO AND JULIET

Critical commentary on *Romeo and Juliet* does not express such a wide divergence of opinion as is common in commentaries dealing with Shakespeare's other plays. This may well be due to the nature of the play itself. The plot constitutes a simple, direct line of action. The agencies directing the action are clearly presented. Characterization, while full of vitality, is not complex, and indeed it need not be. For despite the abundant use of contrasts between love and hate, day and night, youth and old age, conflicts are not realized within the characters themselves. The love that is the subject of the play is too pure and straightforward for that. Still, critical treatment remains indicative of the changes that have occurred in the approach to literature.

One of the earliest critics to consider *Romeo and Juliet* was William Hazlitt, an English man of letters who wrote in the early part of the nineteenth century. Hazlitt's work shows openly the delight of a romantic. To him, the lovers and their passion were ideal, to be appreciated and celebrated in the language of love. The poet Samuel Taylor Coleridge, his contemporary, shared a similar adulation of Shakespeare. His discussion of *Romeo and Juliet* is not as incisive as are many of his critical writings, but Coleridge does go a step further than Hazlitt in making some original comments about the characters. During the major part of the nineteenth century, Shakespeare became the subject of much study and scholarly interest in the universities of Germany. The moralistic attitudes of the times pervade these writings, and on reading them now one often feels that one is reading some type of sermon. Shakespeare was treated as a profound moralist, an aspect of him which does not appear particularly outstanding to us today. Perhaps the best known of the German critics was Gervinus. Gervinus believed that Friar Laurence was Shakespeare's spokesman, and that the play is a discourse on the evil of allowing the passion of love to become the master of reason. If love is dominant, life ends in tragedy. Thus the play becomes a warning to young people, much as it was in Shakespeare's source, Brooke. However, Gervinus did point out Shakespeare's use of the conventions of poetry, and his treatment of the play has its interesting points, despite the moralizing tone. The fullest expression of nineteenth century criticism comes from Edward Dowden, whose keen, intelligent analysis is quite unlike the rhapsodies of Hazlitt. In contrast to Gervinus is the work of a still later critic, Georg Brandes of Denmark. Brandes is not nearly so impressed with the moderate Friar, although he appreciated Laurence as one of Shakespeare's few characters who are at once tranquil and reasonable, and thoroughly beneficent and delightful. Brandes dwells more lengthily on the quality of passion in the play: its innocence, earthiness, paganism, and its instinctive raptures. His depiction of the passion is new and enlightening today.

During the nineteenth century, Shakespeare was admired so wholeheartedly that criticism in its best sense was often replaced by adulation. At the same time, perhaps because the novel was growing in popularity as a form, the characters became the focus of interest in reading the play. Thorough examinations of characters became so much the vogue that whole life histories were sometimes constructed for them. The results of such studies were, at their worst, ridiculous. More often they were irrelevant. But *Romeo and Juliet* was not complicated enough to occasion much critical writing along these lines. The work of Brandes proved to be a major contribution in beginning a new and more rewarding trend of criticism.

Another refreshing reading of Shakespeare was offered in 1947 by Harley Granville-Barker, an actor and director, who because of his intimate involvement with the stage had many provocative insights to offer. He treated the plays as theatre, observing vividly the effects scenes and characters had in production. Throughout the early years of this century, much fine scholarly work was done on the Elizabethan theatre, and this adds still to our understanding of Shakespeare's plays.

Such research gives us a better view of a play as a whole. Perhaps taking his cue from this, H. B. Charlton, a British professor of literature, attempted to form final aesthetic judgments of each play as a separate and complete work. His decision about *Romeo and Juliet* is much concerned with fate. He feels that Shakespeare's craft was still in its experimental stages. Because he sees the tragedy as caused by fate, and because such fate seems unreal to modern audiences, Charlton ultimately finds the play a failure. The role of moral forces in the play is reexamined, in a far less moralistic way, by Stauffer, former professor at Princeton University. He takes the opposite stance from Gervinus, showing the love between Romeo and Juliet to be not morally condemnable but a moving moral power, which teaches the lovers to be themselves and which finally triumphs over death and reconciles hatred.

Other criticism examines closely Shakespeare's language and imagery, shedding light on his meaning through this close analysis. Like all trends in criticism, this can be improperly used, especially is it does not relate to specific plays, their characters and actions. Caroline Spurgeon was a pioneer in the study of imagery, and her book, published in 1935, remains useful in pointing out the trends and connotations of image-patterns throughout the plays. However, her intention to arrive at an understanding of Shakespeare's own personality now seems no less trivial than the earlier works which concocted whole lives for the characters in the plays. The most successful and truly illuminating of these critics, among them G. Wilson Knight and Cleanth Brooks, have not chosen to deal with *Romeo and Juliet* intensively. An excellent work, in which the examination of language and character is somewhat synthesized, is *Shakespeare's Young Lovers,* by E. E. Stoll.

Stoll intends to show that the love and the lovers in the play are dealt with poetically rather than psychologically. They take their vitality and their dimension from poetry, which is suitable to a play in which conflict is not interior. Denis De Rougemont's compelling book, on the other hand, deals with the lovers psychologically as a prototypical couple, who exemplify the destructive romantic love common in this culture. The two points of view are, surprisingly enough, not incompatible, as it is from such extremes of criticism, properly used, that the reader can often cull the widest, richest, and most thought-provoking ideas and insights.

Mark Van Doren is distinguished among the critics of *Romeo and Juliet* for the sympathy of his approach, tempered as it is with keen critical insight. He points up the literary aspects of the play, revealing to us a youthful Shakespeare, in love with words and language. Van Doren impresses this literary quality on his readers through numerous quotations involving words or literature, including Juliet's famous "You kiss by the book." Van Doren also points out the speed of the action, and Shakespeare's technique of inserting forebodings of the play's tragic end. He deals also with the familiar critical matters of the contrasting images of light and dark, day and night, and the lovers' isolation in a world of elders and peers who are incapable of understanding their passion. A further interesting point made by Van Doren in his essay is that Lord Capulet, with his testy naturalness and aged vivacity, is the forerunner of many of Shakespeare's fussy and stubborn old men, notably Polonius in *Hamlet*. The feeling is also expressed that, in an indefinable way, *Romeo and Juliet* is able to engage the attention and understanding of an audience in a particularly intimate manner, the knack of which Shakespeare lost with the growing maturity and changing subject matter evident in his later works.

Alfred Harbage, in his book dealing with Shakespeare and morality, *As They Liked It,* gives us a modern but somewhat different reading of the play. He points up Shakespeare's variations from his source, Brooke, in their differing treatments of the final judgments made on the characters. In Brooke's work, for example, the apothecary who sells Romeo the poison illegally is hung by the neck; the Friar is characterized as a superstitious humbug; and the lovers themselves are condemned for their moral looseness and their disobedience to the dictates of their parents and society. Shakespeare, according to Harbage, gives us the evil, not in these individual instances, but in the society and the feud. He puts emphasis on the Prologue and the final speech by Prince Escalus, making clear the idea that, though the evil in Shakespeare is more general than in Brooke, it is still particularized. The tragedy is due as much to the Capulets and Montagues as it is to chance and fate, if not more. Harbage feels that the ultimate cause of the suffering is concrete and human. In *Romeo and Juliet* it is clearly the senseless strife in which the two families engage. He does not deny the operations of chance but insists that Shakespeare was deeply concerned with the tangible evil as well. Harbage also sheds further light on the recurrent themes in Shakespeare's work in his relating of *Romeo and Juliet* to *King Lear*. He recognizes the comparable effects of chance and fate in both plays, though the power of evil is much stronger in the later and more mature tragedy.

ESSAY QUESTIONS AND ANSWERS

QUESTION

What does Prince Escalus represent, and how does he structure the play?

ANSWER

Prince Escalus is the ruler of Verona. His appearances in the play are formal and stately, and they have a unified purpose: to establish order, enforce law, and mete out justice. He represents the governing forces of humanity: law, order, and justice. He appears at each of the three crucial points in the play: at the beginning, when the feud between the families has broken out anew; at the midpoint of the play, when Mercutio's death has brought about the turning of the action from the romantic to the tragic; and at the very end, when the conflict between the love of the young people and the hatred of their parents has reached its ironic and fateful climax in the lovers' sacrificial death. The Prince's first appearance marks the beginning of the fateful action. He attempts to establish control over the feud by making death the penalty for further fighting. When he comes the second time, the action has made it evident that even the threat of death cannot control this hatred. Even he is suffering then, for one of his own relatives has been killed. When he decrees exile for Romeo, the punishment seems a just one. The Prince little knows how fatal will be the results of the banishment. At the third appearance, the tragedy has occurred, and three young people lie irrevocably dead. The Prince can only do his best to shed some light on the massacre. A far graver punishment than he could have devised has been set down in repudiation of the families' hatred. As a representative of the governing powers of humanity, the Prince has been ineffectual, for fate would have it that love alone can punish hatred. While Prince Escalus's appearances mark nicely the cruxes of the play, the human forces of rational order are shown to be useless weapons against passion. Only fate can mete out higher justice.

QUESTION

To what degree are Mercutio, the Nurse, and the Friar responsible for the tragedy?

ANSWER

Mercutio reacts strongly to Romeo's refusal to respond to
Tybalt's provoking insults. Such a reaction is to be expected
of such a character, for Mercutio's code of honor requires that
provocations of that despicable nature be answered. The
occasion calls for a fight; and when Romeo shows no signs of
giving battle, Mercutio does. His death, however, is virtually
accidental, and it is the accidental death that triggers the
action leading to Romeo's banishment and the subsequent
tragedy. There is nothing in Mercutio's character that can be
held responsible, unless it is that lack of understanding
toward the lovers' passion that he shares with almost all the
other characters in the play.

The Nurse can be blamed somewhat more. Her relation to
Juliet as confidante is comparable to Mercutio's relation to
Romeo. But Romeo does not turn to Mercutio for help. Juliet
does turn to the Nurse, and the Nurse, whose nature is basely
realistic, gives the only response that could be expected of
her. She advises infidelity, a suggestion despicable to the pure-
spirited girl. In advising this, the Nurse lets Juliet down, leaving her no one to turn to but the Friar. Had it been in the
Nurse's nature to propose a simpler solution, such as telling
Juliet's parents the truth, the tragedy might have been avoided.
But such speculations are useless; the Nurse is responsible by
default, because of her innate nature.

The Friar, confidant to both Romeo and Juliet, plays a more
integral and deliberate part in the action leading to tragedy. It
is he that condones and performs the secret marriage. It is he
that gives Juliet the crucial sleeping poison and accepts the
responsibility for informing Romeo of this state of events. Both
actions might be objectively judged foolish, but they were

done with the best intentions to reconcile the feud and help the lovers. He causes the deaths far more directly than either Mercutio or the Nurse, but he cannot be held ultimately responsible. It is a fateful accident that the message does not get through. In the final analysis, only fate and the fated quality of the love can be blamed.

QUESTION
How does love function as a teacher in the play?

ANSWER
At the beginning of the play, Romeo is a callow youth, in love with love, and affecting the postures of love as he has learned them from books. Juliet is a sweet and docile child, bound still to her parents and willing to try to answer their requests in the affirmative. Neither lover has established a personal character, but love teaches both of them to be themselves. Romeo discovers that joy, far from being incompatible with love, is inseparable from it. He gains the strength first to accept and then to deal with obstacles to his desire. In the end, love has taught him that he can defy fate, can promptly sum up the meaning and fortune of his life and take it into his own hands. He feels older than Paris, though they are contemporaries. Death becomes his triumph, all for the sake of love. In Juliet, loves causes the capacity for practicality (including necessary deception) to increase; her imagination, capacity for emotion, and strength blossom as well. In her final scene before taking the sleeping potion, these last three show themselves fully developed. She, like Romeo, can choose death as the only means to triumph in love.

But love has a wider effect than that of bringing maturity to the lovers. Shakespeare has deliberately made it the rectifying influence on the entire play. The Prologue predicted that only the death of the lovers would end the feud. In the final scene, when just this has come about, Prince Escalus says to the heads of the two households, "See what a scourge is laid upon your hate,/ That heaven finds means to kill your joys with love." Society has needed an example of love in order to rectify hatred, and love is shown to have moral power. There is an even more central meaning to the play than this. Love is triumphant over death, over time, and over fate, as well as over hatred. The primary emotional lesson learned from the play is that love of such quality is a lasting ideal, not a merely temporary passion.

QUESTION

Trace the imagery of explosion, showing how it works as a theme as well as an image.

ANSWER

Romeo and Juliet choose their own fate in choosing their love. Such love is impetuous and bound to end in destruction. It is explosively dangerous, and the images of explosion not only describe the passion, but often link it with warnings and forebodings of a violent conclusion. The mild Friar cautions Romeo: "Love moderately: long love doth so;/ Too swift arrives as tardy as too slow." Advice such as this is alien and inadmissible to the lovers. They glory in exactly those aspects of their love that the Friar admonishes. The very beauty of the love is that it is a light in darkness, a brilliance in the night. Juliet's eyes seem to her lover brighter than the stars. The lovers rely on the beauty of their bodies to provide enough illumination for them during their secret meetings. Yet during their first courting, Juliet is a little frightened of the love: "It is too rash, too unadvis'd, too sudden;/ Too like the lightning which doth cease to be/ Ere one can say 'It lightens.'" She senses, and gives expression to the danger, and her image is of lightning that explodes brightly but disappears before it can even be talked about. It is she who thus begins the image, and the Friar picks it up in a more warning tone when he says to Romeo: "These violent delights have violent ends/ And in their triumph die, like fire and powder,/ Which, as they kiss, consume." The vague danger of Juliet's words is more vivid and pressing in this speech, and the explosion imagery is fully realized. The Friar means his words as a warning. When considered more abstractly, this description epitomizes the love. It is such a love that it must explode triumphantly and die in one quick instant. The imagery of explosion characterizes the love and its necessary end, bringing together the related imagery of light and dark. Light and dark become more and more identified with each other, just as the love and death, of which these images are symbolic, grow together. The result of light and dark, love and death becoming one, is explosion: As love and death kiss, they consume. The result is the disaster in the tomb. Thus explosion becomes emblematic of the subject matter and action of the play, assuming the attributes of a theme, and figuring largely in our understanding of the climactic tragedy.

BIBLIOGRAPHY

BACKGROUND OF IDEAS

The following books analyze the philosophies of the Renaissance and the culture and mindset of the Elizabethans.

Bradbrook, Muriel Clara, *The Artist and Society in Shakespeare's England* (Totowa, NJ: Barnes & Noble, 1982).

Cook, Ann Jennalie, *Making a Match: Courtship in Shakespeare and His Society* (Princeton: Princeton University Press, 1991).

Haydn, Hiram, *The Counter-Renaissance* (New York: Scribner, 1950).

Kay, Dennis, *William Shakespeare: His Life and Times* (New York: Twayne Publishers, 1995).

Mallin, Eric Scott, *Inscribing the Time: Shakespeare and the End of Elizabethan England* (Berkeley: University of California Press, 1995).

McMurty, Jo, *Understanding Shakespeare's England: A Companion for the American Reader* (Hamden, CT: Archon Books, 1989).

Morse, David, *England's Time of Crisis: From Shakespeare to Milton: A Cultural History* (New York: St. Martin's Press, 1989).

Papp, Joseph, and Elizabeth Kirkland, *Shakespeare Alive!* (New York: Bantam Books, 1988).

Rowse, Alfred Leslie, *The Elizabethan Renaissance* (New York: Scribner, 1972).

Shuger, Debora K., *Habits of Thought in the English Renaissance: Religion, Politics, and the Dominant Culture* (Berkeley: University of California Press, 1990).

Spencer, Hazelton, *The Art and Life of William Shakespeare* (New York: Harcourt, Brace, 1940).

Tillyard, E. M. W., *The Elizabethan World Picture* (London: Chatto and Windus, 1952).

MAJOR CRITICAL WORKS, PAST AND PRESENT
Bradley, Andrew C., *Shakespearean Tragedy* (New York: Meridian Books, 1955). A major study of Shakespeare's tragedies, especially good on character analysis.

Champion, Larry S. *The Essential Shakespeare: An Annotated Bibliography of Major Modern Studies* (New York: Maxwell Macmillan International, 1993).

Charlton, Henry Buckley, *Romeo and Juliet as an Experimental Tragedy* (London: Humphrey Milford, 1940).

Charlton, Henry Buckley, *Shakespearean Tragedy* (Cambridge: Cambridge University Press, 1961).

Coleridge, Samuel Taylor, *Coleridge's Shakespearean Criticism* (Cambridge, 1930, and in many reprints). Valuable for the critical insights of one who was himself a great poet.

Dowden, Edward, Shakespeare: *A Critical Study of His Mind and Art* (New York: Harpers, 1918).

Empson, William, *Essays on Shakespeare* (New York: Cambridge University Press, 1986).

Frye, Northrop, *Northrop Frye on Shakespeare* (New Haven: Yale University Press, 1986). Collection of university lectures.

Granville-Barker, Harley, *Prefaces to Shakespeare* (Princeton: Princeton University Press, 1947, two volumes). The classic work on Shakespeare's stagecraft and on the plays in actual performance, by a famous producer of Shakespearean plays.

Greer, Germaine, *Shakespeare* (New York: Oxford University Press, 1986).

Hazlitt, William, *Characters of Shakespeare's Plays* (London, 1870, and often reprinted). Insights of one of the greatest Romantic critics.

Knight, G. Wilson, *The Wheel of Fire* (New York: Meridian Books, 1957). Intensely poetic and interesting reading of the play.

Kott, Jan, *Shakespeare, Our Contemporary* (Garden City, New York: Doubleday, 1964). A groundbreaking work that has done much to shape modern presentations of Shakespeare.

Lamb, Charles, "On the Tragedies of Shakespeare," in *The Works of Charles Lamb* (London, 1818, and in many reprints). Very influential criticism.

Marowitz, Charles, *Recycling Shakespeare* (New York: Applause Theatre Book Publishers, 1991). "This book is directed at two enemies—the academics and the traditionalists," Marowitz begins; he goes on to examine a variety of aspects of Shakespearean criticism and performance with a unique style and with provocative insights.

Nicoll, Allardyce, *Studies in Shakespeare* (New York: Harcourt, Brace, 1927).

Spencer, Theodore, *Shakespeare and the Nature of Man* (New York: The Macmillan Co., 1949).

Spurgeon, Caroline, *Shakespeare's Imagery* (London: Cambridge University Press, 1935). Influential study of Shakespeare's similes and metaphors and on their influence upon dramatic meaning.

Stavig, Mark, *The Form of Things Unknown: Renaissance Metaphor in Romeo and Juliet and A Midsummer Night's Dream* (Pittsburgh: Duquesne University Press, 1995).

Stoll, E. E. *Art and Artifice in Shakespeare* (Cambridge: Cambridge University Press, 1933). The thesis of this book (which does not treat specifically of *Romeo and Juliet*) is that characters should be viewed in terms of the actual performance of the drama.

Swinburne, Algernon C., *Three Plays of Shakespeare* (London: Harper, 1909). Especially interesting on religious attitudes in *Lear,* by an outstanding 19th-century poet.

Tolstoy, Leo, *Tolstoy on Shakespeare* (New York: Funk & Wagnalls, 1906). A hostile, provocative, and intensely personal interpretation by the great novelist. It should be read in connection with George Orwell's "Lear, Tolstoy and the Fool," in *Shooting an Elephant* (London: Secker & Warburg, 1950).

Traversi, D. A., *An Approach to Shakespeare* (New York: Doubleday Anchor, 1956). One of the most stimulating twentieth-century interpretations.

Van Doren, Mark, *Shakespeare* (New York: Doubleday Anchor, 1953). A sane, simple approach.

Watts, Cedric Thomas. *Romeo and Juliet* (Boston: Twayne Publishers, 1991).

Zesmer, David M. *Guide to Shakespeare* (New York: Barnes & Noble, 1976). Excellent presentation of backgrounds, summaries, and interpretations of Shakespearean drama and poetry.

ANTHOLOGIES OF CRITICISM

In addition to the following anthologies, you might want to examine journals that anthologize Shakespearean criticism— for example, *Shakespeare Quarterly, Shakespeare Studies,* and *Shakespeare Survey.*

Calderwood, James L., and Harold E. Toliver, eds., *Essays in Shakespearean Criticism* (Englewood Cliffs, NJ: Prentice-Hall, 1970).

Cole, Douglas, ed., *Twentieth Century Interpretations of Romeo and Juliet: A Collection of Critical Essays* (Englewood Cliffs, NJ: Prentice-Hall, 1970).

Smith, D. N. *Shakespeare Criticism: A Selection* (London: Oxford University Press, 1961).

STAGE PRODUCTION

The following books examine Shakespearean theater—the Globe itself, actors and acting, technical aspects of production, and the audience.

Adams, John Cranford, *The Globe Playhouse: Its Design and Equipment* (New York: Barnes & Noble, 1961).

De Banke, Cecile, *Shakespearean Stage Production: Then and Now* (New York: McGraw-Hill, 1953).

Gurr, Andrew, *Playgoing in Shakespeare's London* (New York: Cambridge University Press, 1987).

Gurr, Andrew, *Rebuilding Shakespeare's Globe* (New York: Routledge, 1989).

Hodges, C. Walter, *The Globe Restored: A Study of the Elizabethan Theatre* (New York: Coward-McCann, 1968).

Orrell, John, *The Quest for Shakespeare's Globe* (New York: Cambridge University Press, 1983).

NOTES

NOTES

NOTES

NOTES

NOTES

NOTES

NOTES

NOTES

NOTES

NOTES

NOTES